Get Out of My Bed

Shirley Wooten Rose

Copyright 2018 © Shirley Wooten Rose

No part of this book may be reproduced, or transmitted in any form or by any means, electronic or mechanical, including photocopying, recording, or by any information storage and retrieval system, without the written permission of the author or publisher.

Publishing Services: One Smart Lady Productions
http://onesmartladyproductions.org

For more information:
One Smart Lady Productions
Publishing Services
info@onesmartladyproductions.org

Cover Photo by Marcus Cramer on unsplash.com

First Edition

Imprint: Independently Published
ISBN: 978-1723991-5-78

Printed in United States of America

10 9 8 7 6 5 4 3 2 1

Dedication

This memoir is dedicated to my awesome daughters, who have grown into intelligent, successful young women. They have certainly been through many of life's challenges with me. I have made my share of mistakes along the way, which made an impression on their own personal development. But, regardless of my sometimes making a wrong turn, they were always respectful and well-behaved girls. They never gave me any major problems or concerns. I am very proud to be their mom and my wish for them is to be happy and enjoy their life. I love spending time with them and hope the future holds many enjoyable, fun memories.

Table of Contents

Dedication
Preface ..... i-iv

Chapters

  1 - More Good than Bad 1
  2 - Keeping Tom Happy 8
  3 - I Begin to Crumble 14
  4 - Seeking Help 23
  5 - Breaking Away 26
  6 - Liar, Cheat and Thief 43
  7 - Patronizing Tom 54
  8 - Keeping the Peace 62
  9 - Unsafe Desperation 69
  10- Divorce Another Story 75
  11- Out of Control 88
  12- Twice A Victim 108
  13- Tom's List of Debts 120
  14- My Monetary Contribution 130
  15- The Fee Dispute 135
  16- Happy Trails 138

Message from Shirley Rose 141

Preface

I opened the refrigerator door and began to laugh. My husband Paul smiled and asked what was so funny. I replied that in my previous life it was unbelievable how many tongue lashings I endured over an appliance as simple as a refrigerator.

My list of sins could be lengthy, and if one of the following was noted by my ex-husband upon his arrival home, I would be appropriately reprimanded. My offenses might include:

1. All ice trays should be filled to the rim and placed under those already frozen.

2. Freezer area should be spotless and free of any frost accumulation.

3. No frozen meats should show signs of freezer burn.

4. Never leave a liter bottle containing a small amount of liquid in the fridge.

Get Out of My Bed

5. Never leave two identical products.

6. The smaller products should not be placed on the tall shelf.

7. Never put a half-filled drink cup in the refrigerator thinking you'll finish it later.

8. Make sure all cheese shows no sign of being moldy--especially the type of mold which could be a new source of penicillin.

9. Heaven help you if there's green slime growing on any green veggies in the crisper.

10. Make sure you clean the top of the refrigerator twice a week and make sure it's free of any so-called clutter.

On occasion, Tom would run his fingers across the top of the fridge and ask me when I was going to plant it. My reply was always, "I think petunias would look very nice there."

I can laugh about my failure to live up to this man's expectations because there was no way I could meet his demands. No matter how spotless our home was--if Tom was in one of his moods, I didn't stand a chance of pleasing him. I was doomed to be on the receiving end of a demeaning lecture. This was only one of his many subconscious tactics to reduce me to a depressed, sullen female. Before my marriage to Tom, I was a very optimistic, fun-loving woman--dedicated to pleasing and caring for my family.

It was extremely frustrating to find that the harder I worked to please my husband the farther I seemed to slip from his graces. I would rush to get home before he did so that I could rectify anything in the house that I knew would irritate him.

My two teenage daughters from my previous marriage also lived with us and they were a tremendous help with the normal household chores. The girls were very respectful of Tom and did not cause us any major behavior problems, but when Tom arrived home they knew not to be caught doing something frivolous such as listening to the radio, watching TV or taking a nap.

It now turns my stomach to think how the three of us walked on eggshells to keep the peace with this man. The last two years of our marriage I pleaded with him to go to a marriage counselor but he flatly refused until it was too late. Even when he finally agreed to go, he only went three times and refused to go again. I gave him every chance conceivable for him to understand what he was doing to us and our relationship.

Get Out of My Bed

My pleas fell on deaf ears. His reply was always, "I don't understand what your problem is, Shirley. You have a beautiful home, a cabin in the woods, we both make good money and your husband loves you more than anyone else ever could." I would reply, "But look at the way you treat me!" He could never understand what I meant. When he finally realized that I was really considering leaving him and I forced him to see a counselor, his abuse became physical.

The tension and stress I endured in this marriage will never be forgotten. I actually became physically ill from trying to deal with Tom and if I can save one person from entering an abusive relationship, by writing this book, then the time and effort spent will be well worth it.

It also has been a healing process to write this incredible story. My personal commitment to accomplish this task has helped to heal some of the tremendous frustration and pain that I still carry. I am extremely happy in my present life and thank God that I found my new partner. I have peace and control of my destiny once again, and I definitely feel loved and respected, which is most important of all.

"Love Should Not Hurt"

Chapter 1
More Good than Bad

Tom and I were married in November of 1979 in a small private ceremony. A few friends from Tom's place of employment, my daughters, and two of my closest friends attended. Tom and I had only met five months before and it had been a short, whirlwind romance.

The first two years of the marriage Tom was very attentive, loving and supportive. We played hard and worked hard. Tom is a very intelligent person and I was always impressed with his ability to repair just about anything whether mechanical or otherwise. He is a very meticulous, organized person and made every minute of the day count.

Initially, he listened to what the girls and I had to say, and the communication was great. Each evening around nine o'clock Tom and I would sit in the kitchen,

Get Out of My Bed

have a snack and discuss the day's events and plans for the future. I truly felt we had a great relationship, and nothing would ever come between us. I was determined that we would live happily ever after.

Tom and I were both very busy in our careers. Tom was a plastics engineer and I had begun a new sales position with a pharmaceutical company.

We had very little time to spend socially, therefore our lives centered around our home, work, and my two daughters, who were 13 and 14 years of age. I had never been successful in obtaining any financial or emotional support from the girls' father, so I had resolved myself to being their sole support. They had always been very good children and I have never had any major problems with them even during my unsettling marriage to Tom.

Tom had three children from his first marriage: two sons and a daughter. The daughter was still in college being supported by Tom, while the sons were grown and self-supporting. During the seven years, we were married, I only saw his daughter twice. On several occasions, I asked Tom why they didn't spend more time together. His answer was that she did not approve of our marriage. This is called a "Pass the Buck" answer, and one which I would get many times

More Good Than Bad

over the next few years. We did spend some quality time with his two sons with whom I felt we had a fairly close relationship. But on one occasion Tom's younger son, Kirt, expressed very negative feelings about his father. He was visiting with us one afternoon when the girls came home from school. They both greeted Tom with a hug and kiss as they always did and Tom appeared to be affectionate toward them. I was told in private that this was not the father that Kirt knew and that he hoped that I would never know that person.

I was very surprised at what he had said, but in the back of my mind, I also knew other members of Tom's family had made similar comments. More than once I had been told that I was the best thing that had ever happened to him and they could not believe the change in his personality. These comments were confusing to me, but I didn't dwell on them since we were getting along fine.

Tom, so far, had been a very loving, compassionate companion. I felt that possibly he had been difficult with people because he was unhappy in his previous marriage. I was certainly not having any problems in our relationship.

Over the next few months, there were a few small incidents which I would describe as irritating, but not

Get Out of My Bed

maddening. On occasion, Tom would not take my advice. In other words, he seemed to not value my opinion on what I describe as simple, common sense issues. For example, we argued once over whether or not we could put corn husks down the garbage disposal. I asked him not to put them through the disposal and he insisted it was okay. We had company arriving for dinner within the hour and I asked him again to please not use it. He refused to listen to me and fifteen minutes before our guests arrived he still had his head under the sink trying to dislodge the husks.

Another time we were taking down our Christmas tree and I asked him to please wait for me to get a sheet. I wanted to carry the tree out on the sheet so we would not get needles in the carpet. He refused to wait and I was cleaning pine needles out of our white shag carpet for the next three months.

I can recall more than one plastic or wooden kitchen utensil which was destroyed when Tom insisted on putting it in the dishwasher. All the while I would be standing beside him asking that he not place them in the washer. And when the melted or discolored item would be pulled from the washer, I never received an apology or heard him say, "You were right."

More Good Than Bad

These are small incidents but are important when we speak of basic communication and respect.

The first time I saw the dark, moody side of Tom came like a thunderbolt from nowhere. It was eight months after our marriage and I was cooking on the outdoor grill when he came home from work. Instead of his normal hug and kiss, I was greeted by a very cutting remark about something fairly unimportant. His remark and attitude were totally out of character for the man I knew as my husband. Being in a good mood, I laughed and said, "Lighten up, don't be such a grouch." He glared at me and said in a tone I had never heard from him, "Don't ever call me that again. That's what my ex-wife used to call me!" I was totally shocked at his behavior and totally confused as to what the hell had just happened. I was feeling great, looking forward to my husband's arrival and now I was very hurt and upset over what? Had I said or done something to deserve this? The answer is no, but that didn't make the pain I felt any less. I took refuge in our bedroom for the next hour until I could settle down and try to figure out how not to let this happen again. I searched for excuses. Had he had a terrible day at work and simply taken it out on me?

Get Out of My Bed

The answer is that I had just seen the other Tom that I had heard bits and pieces about from other family members. But being the optimistic, good-natured female that I am, I was determined to make this marriage work and this man happy. I knew there had to be more good in the person than bad, and I was willing to do what I could to inspire the loving, congenial side to Tom.

This is a great philosophy and attitude as long as you don't lose your self-esteem and sanity in the process.

Unfortunately, when I took the big step and married Tom, I had no idea this type of Jekyll/Hyde personality existed. Even though I majored in sociology and psychology in college, I was unaware that how this person treated me at the beginning of the relationship would slowly change. I had come from the old school of judging a person by the way he or she treated me only. But in a romantic relationship, this simply is not good enough.

If you don't seriously consider every aspect of this person's life before you join in Holy matrimony with him/her, it may come back to haunt you. You can help reduce the chances of entering into an unhealthy relationship by spending a lot of time with the person

More Good Than Bad

in many different social situations. Be aware of any inconsistencies in your conversations. If s/he tells you one thing today and something totally different a week from now. You have a problem.

Chapter 2
Keeping Tom Happy

The change in Tom's personality was very gradual. By the third year together there were still lots of good times, but I found myself on the defensive in order to keep from dealing with Tom's dark side.

Our lives were extremely busy and between a very demanding career, spending quality time with my daughters, and seeing that Tom was a happy husband, there was no time left. It became a treadmill existence. When I look back now and see how I juggled my everyday life, I certainly don't want to ever do it again. But keeping Tom from throwing one of his temper tantrums was like trying to fill a gallon bucket with a thimble. It was simply impossible to do.

The girls were a tremendous help in keeping the house clean and daily chores done. We made lists of all the things that needed to be accomplished. It was

Keeping Tom Happy

a large home and we had to keep on top of it every day. Our list of chores seemed to have an unwritten meaning between the lines which spelled "How to keep Tom happy." In other words, how to keep either the girls or myself from becoming the recipient of one of Tom's verbal attacks. But no matter how spotless our house was, it was never good enough for Tom.

I always tried to get home from work before him so that I could do a spot check of things that, if not done, might set him off. My checklist consisted of trash emptied, no dirty dishes in the sink, all beds made, no clothing lying on the floor or furniture, nothing laid on tables such as newspapers or magazines, top of the refrigerator was clean and uncluttered, and so on and so on. But the very sad, depressing part of the entire scenario was that no matter how hard we worked to meet the standards Tom set if he was in one of his moods, he would find something to lecture one of us about. Everyone including myself made sure that they were doing something Tom considered constructive when he walked through the door. And I can assure you that if you tried to explain or defend yourself you just made matters worse. The lectures would include telling you how the job should have been done, how you failed to pay attention to detail, or that almost doing it right doesn't count.

Get Out of My Bed

We soon learned that to try to discuss the situation was hopeless and that the best way to handle it was to simply agree and get it over with. Tom obviously has an overwhelming need to control and manipulate anyone around him. Life became a game of just trying to stay out of the direct line of fire from his verbal attacks, especially when he was in one of his moods.

But knowing when he might lash out at us over nothing was another guessing game. From day to day we never knew what the atmosphere would be at the dinner table. He could be very congenial and mellow or in a split second, he could turn into a fire-spitting dragon. And the same thing that set him off today might not even faze him tomorrow. I could discuss an issue with him today and feel we had agreed and that the problem was solved but bring it up tomorrow and he might act like we never even discussed it. There were no set rules of logic that we could hang our hats on. We were totally at his emotional mercy every day. We began to feel that he was very systematically trying to drive us crazy.

Tom made his rules by the hour and it depended on what side of the fence he was on that particular day as to whether his answer was black or white, yes or no, etc.

Keeping Tom Happy

It was the most unstable, maddening, psychological atmosphere I have ever known or ever want to know.

He had lots of "Just Because I Said So" rules, one of which was that no one goes barefoot in our home even if it's 100 degrees outside. Fortunately, I never lost my sense of humor, for on a hot summer afternoon I caught one of my daughters walking around barefooted. I placed two fingers across my upper lip and mimicked Hitler and started chasing her around our kitchen. I was screaming at her, "You vill vear shoes! You vill vear shoes!" We were both laughing hysterically but stopped short when we saw Tom glaring at us. He asked what we were doing in his very stern manner. I replied, "Just having a little fun."

This person I found myself married to was not what I thought I was getting. It was like being married to two different people. He could be very loving and happy one minute and the next to be attacking me with whatever verbal nasties he could dream up. I often thought it was like a demon hiding some place in this man's psyche that at any given moment, for no apparent reason, just simply appeared. My entire existence was a maze of responses to Tom. I was living in an atmosphere in which I felt I had no control whatsoever.

Get Out of My Bed

I'll never forget a morning when I was getting ready to go to work and I got a spoon lodged in the garbage disposal. I was the only one in the house. While I worked to dislodge it, I could just hear Tom's voice screaming in my ear, "How many times have I told you not to put silverware on that side of the sink? As a matter of fact, there shouldn't be any dirty silverware on either side of the sink! It should be in the dishwasher!" I literally broke out in a sweat while trying to free this spoon and there was no way I would let Tom find it there that evening. I would not put myself in the position of being on the receiving end of one of his lectures. I finally dislodged the spoon and at the same moment realized how totally ridiculous the whole scene was--to be that afraid of being reprimanded by another human being was sick.

I was responding to this man like he was a tyrannical father rather than a loving husband. The emotional support and approval that we all need from our spouses were nonexistent.

On several occasions when I tried to communicate with him in an attempt to find out why he appeared to be so miserable and unhappy, I was only met with his disbelief that there was anything wrong in our relationship. His answer was that something must

Keeping Tom Happy

be wrong with me since no one could love me more than he. Not to mention the fact that I have a beautiful home, a cabin in the woods, and anything I want. So obviously I must be the one with the problem.

Chapter 3
I Begin to Crumble

    By the fourth year of our marriage, I was becoming both mentally and physically exhausted. The atmosphere in our home could be described as an emotional minefield. In other words, the girls and I tiptoed on eggshells in order to avoid a critical encounter with Tom. It had become very apparent that no matter how hard we worked to meet his standards, he would not only refuse to acknowledge a job well done but find an area in which he could complain. It was a very depressing no-win situation. I wasn't really aware at the time as to how my own self-esteem was suffering from this relationship. I often wonder whether or not Tom understands how he treats his loved ones or if he is totally unaware of his actions. Either way, the pain which he inflicts on others is still the same.

    As I searched for answers to deal with Tom's moods, not only did I begin to suffer emotionally, but my problems became physical as well. I awoke one

I Begin to Crumble

night with excruciating pain in my neck and shoulders. No matter how I turned in bed or tried to get relief, nothing worked. I finally got out of bed and paced the floor for hours crying like a baby.

Dr. Susan Forward, in her book, <u>Men Who Hate Women and the Women Who Love Them</u>, addresses the problems caused by anger unconsciously directed inward. She states that stress can show up in the musculoskeletal system as backaches, muscle spasms, general body tightness, and/or tension headaches. It may also manifest itself in the digestive tract. I also had stomach problems and would have to run for the restroom immediately after eating.

After having the muscle spasms in my back, I visited a chiropractor numerous times but did not seem to get any relief. I finally decided that maybe more physical exercise was the answer since I spent all day driving in my job. I informed Tom that I would like to join an exercise class. His reply was that he did not want me undressing in front of those other people.

We were having dinner with friends and very little was said about it the remainder of the evening. But when we returned home we had a terrible argument and he took me out to breakfast the next morning to discuss it further. I would not back down and informed him that

Get Out of My Bed

if I wanted to join an exercise class I would. He saw that I was adamant and finally said to go ahead. My question is why do I have to go through such a hassle in order to join an exercise class? I would think that a husband would be glad if a wife were trying to take better care of herself. But in order to get his approval, I had to go through a lengthy discussion and explain to him that I felt it would help relieve the pain in my back since nothing else had worked. I was once again having to explain myself--which I spent a lot of time doing around Tom. No matter what the subject was, from the most trivial to more important, I often found myself explaining or rationalizing in order for him to understand me. I felt like a ten-year-old talking to her father in order to gain approval. I would get extremely frustrated with him and want to scream at him that I was not a child, I had a brain, and to just give me a break. And if he saw I was getting upset he would tell me I was too sensitive.

I think the only way I was able to stay in this marriage as long as I did was because I had changed jobs and was now on the road four or five nights a month. Tom was traveling also. Therefore, the time spent with one another was usually limited. I knew the situation was becoming critical, but I really did not

I Begin to Crumble

want another divorce. When I married Tom, I was so sure that this was it and we would be together forever. I felt life had played a very dirty trick on me and I kept trying to make things right.

By this time the girls were teenagers and quite self-sufficient. We had very few problems with them, so when Tom and I went to our cabin on weekends the girls stayed at home. They would go skiing with us during the winter, but for the most part, we went alone. I looked forward to Friday nights and getting away for the weekend.

Our cabin was located in the country on a back-dirt road and we had a lot of peace and quiet. But sometimes during that three-hour ride to camp, I could get myself into a lot of trouble by simply making idle conversation. I recall one particular Friday night when it was late fall and it began to snow. We were in our pick-up truck and I asked if we had snow tires. Tom informed me that we had all-weather radial tires and since I had driven the truck many times could not understand why I was unaware of that fact. He proceeded to give me a lengthy lecture on my lack of attention to detail. We were only 20 minutes from camp when this discussion arose. When we arrived at the cabin, I was fit to be tied. I did not want to be in the

Get Out of My Bed

same room with the man, much less in the same bed. I had been in a great mood 30 minutes before, and now I was in a rage.

On another Friday night drive, the normally four-lane highway became a two-lane because of construction. Therefore, Tom was unable to pass the car in front of him for several miles. He was riding the car's bumper so closely that I could not even see it. I did not utter a word because I knew it would not make any difference if I did. The passenger in the car turned around and glared at us, especially since we were in a truck and they were driving a small compact. The situation finally resolved itself with no accident and we continued. Later in the drive, Tom asked me to take the wheel since he had stopped for an ice cream cone. I really did not want to because I knew there would be an argument and sure enough there was.

Tom became very irritated because I was driving the speed limit of 55 mph. He started harassing me by saying that we were never going to get there if I didn't speed up. He kept after me, trying to get me to speed, but I wouldn't. He told me that he would pay my ticket if I got caught. I told him that was a really nice gesture but that I would be the one who would get the points on my license. Since I drive a company

I Begin to Crumble

car, that would look great on my record. He kept after me until I couldn't take it another minute. I started screaming at him. I told him that there was no way I was going to speed and that if he wanted to drive he could take the wheel. I said, "How dare you say a word about my driving when you could have caused a major accident a few minutes ago by riding that guy's tail so closely." But nothing I ever said seemed to affect him. I could approach an issue with Tom very calmly or I could blow up when he pushed me over the edge. Either way, it never seemed to matter. There simply was no way to reach this man. Once again, I had been looking forward to the weekend, but now I simply did not care one way or another. Once again, he had made me miserable. The only enjoyable moments I had during the last few years of the marriage was during the snowmobiling season. I loved the sport and had taken to it like a duck takes to water. But even those fun times were marred by Tom's verbal attacks.

I once asked him to ride my sled because I felt something was mechanically wrong. He rode it for a few minutes, gave it back to me, and said, "There's nothing wrong with your sled. Just get on the damn thing and ride it." An hour later the clutch died.

Get Out of My Bed

On one beautiful snowy day, several of us were riding together and everyone was getting stuck because the snow was so deep. I could see that Tom was off his sled and waving his arms at me, but I couldn't hear what he was saying. I pulled up a little ahead of him and stopped in order to hear what he was saying. I was shocked when I realized that Tom was screaming at me, asking why I stopped. I just looked at him in disbelief that he was being such a jerk, especially in front of our friends. The girl riding behind me pulled up and heard him screaming. She asked me why I didn't tell him to go to hell. My reply was that I would when the time was right. That was one of the very few times that Tom allowed any of our friends to see his dark side.

On another occasion, we were in a group and had to ride up a very steep hill. We always climbed this hill one at a time because invariably someone couldn't make it, either because it was so icy, their sled simply didn't have the power, or the rider didn't gun it enough at the bottom. Tom was in the lead as usual and I was second. Tom made the hill. But when I tried, I got within two feet of the top and couldn't go any further. I was so close that I just grabbed my brake because I knew the guys could just pull me up the other five feet. Tom looked down at me from the top of the hill and said, "You let me down again." I can't count the

I Begin to Crumble

number of times that men have praised my ability on a sled and said, "I wish my wife could ride like you do." And here my husband is telling me I have failed miserably. It doesn't matter to him that my sled doesn't have the power that the others do or that because of the icy conditions it's difficult to make the hill. I can't explain to you how furious I was. We were on our way to breakfast and I didn't speak another word to him until later in the day. The group had stopped at a local bar to have a drink and one of the men told Tom that if he spoke to his wife like Tom spoke to me she would divorce him. Tom's reply was, "That's how you make a man out of her." I replied, "I'm already 99% male, so you'd better hope I keep the 1% female hot."

On one occasion, Tom was leading a group of guys we had never met before. I was bringing up the rear and I know the person in front of me did not know if I was a man or woman, because of the gear we wear. Not that it would have made any difference. Normal snowmobiling courtesy is to always keep the person behind you in your sights for safety reasons, etc. I got stuck in a creek and the guy in front of me never realized I was no longer behind him. Another group came along and helped me get my sled back on the trail. I took another trail to our destination and I was sitting at the bar when Tom and his group arrived.

Get Out of My Bed

When Tom walked in, I yelled at him, "Hey, Tom, remember me, your wife?" He said, "How did you do that?" I replied, I got stuck in the creek and that guy behind you owes me a beer because he ran off and left me. He was totally clueless about my whereabouts or safety.

Chapter 4
Seeking Help

During 1984 I became more desperate in my efforts to make Tom understand what was happening to our marriage. The more I tried to communicate with him the more adamant he became in his disbelief that there was anything wrong. His response was that he didn't understand why I was unhappy when no one could love me more than he did. My reply would be, "But you treat me like dirt." He would always brush it off stating that I was just too sensitive. I rationalized with him that if I felt this way, why couldn't he at least make some effort to understand why, especially since I was his wife. I never had any success in getting through to him.

In the spring of 1985, I contacted my company's human resource department and they gave me the name of a marriage counselor. I begged Tom to go with me, but he flatly refused. I was absolutely miserable and had to talk to someone. I knew in my gut that I was

GET OUT OF MY BED

right in the way I felt but I needed a third party to confirm that I wasn't the one who was insane here. The counselor was a lady in her fifties with a very pleasant and motherly air about her. I explained to her how unhappy I was in my marriage and that I could not communicate with my husband. I told her how I never knew from one day to the next what his reaction would be to a given situation, and that he kept me totally confused as to how he felt about me and what he expected from me as a wife and companion. One day things could be fine and the next he would make me feel like an incompetent idiot.

She assured me that my feelings and concerns were justifiable and asked me to be more assertive in explaining myself to Tom. I left her office feeling a new surge of energy and inspiration to save my marriage.

For the next few months I did everything but stand on my head to get Tom's attention, but no such luck. The more I tried to talk to him the more defensive and argumentative he became and we would simply end the conversation by screaming at one another. I felt more and more alone and desperate. I begged him once again to see a marriage counselor. I told him that if he just wanted to go alone and speak to someone to please do so. He flatly refused and told me, "We don't need an outsider to solve our problems."

Seeking Help

I went to the marriage counselor one more time during 1985, which helped me psychologically, but could not find any answers to resolve my dilemma with Tom.

Chapter 5
Breaking Away

In January of 1986, the company I was selling for offered me the territory where our weekend cabin was located. Both Tom and I had hoped to eventually retire in this area and I knew I had to take the offer or I may not get the opportunity again, especially if I wanted to stay with the same company. Both of the girls were either in college or working so my decision would not affect them. So, we leased our home, Tom rented an apartment near his present job, and I moved to the cabin to take over the new territory. Tom's eventual plan was to locate a new job within the next year near our camp. Tom drove up to the cabin on weekends and was able to stay over some during the week when he was making calls in the area. Even though we were spending less time together, our relationship became more tense.

In the spring I took a drastic measure and left him for four days. He had no idea where I had gone or

Breaking Away

when I would be back. When I finally returned he was hysterical. During the time I was gone, Tom wrote the following letter:

Tues eve
3/11/86

Dear Shirley,

    I have enclosed a picture of a lady I love more than I can say. My wish is to see her as happy and as free as the animals she loves. I will do whatever it takes to make this so. I ask you to forgive my ignorance and to grant me the chance to make up for all of my stupidity. I will lay myself at your feet and listen to your words. You are a good person--one of the best I have ever known. If anything, ever happened to you I would take care of you forever. We have worked so hard together and I let my job make me lose sight of the most important things in my life. We can finish the house and you can live as you want. I can adjust to any kind of life you want if you will stay my wife. I have been under great stress with bills and work but that is no excuse for my bad manners. You always did your share and gave so much of yourself to all. The bills are resolved for now and I can see an end to them soon. We can save for an easy life later. We still have the girls to look after and I want to help them. They are nice and I love them both. I know I was hard on them but I wanted them to be tops. No matter how you decide I will always love you all. A man cannot ever give up his family. I have not known God as such but I have asked for his help now. Please find it in your heart to ask me to come to you Friday night. I will not do anything to upset you. Give me the chance to see you each weekend for a few weeks as you search for what you want. We came together for a reason and I will honor that reason. There is so much we can do if you will take the lead and guide me in the proper way. For all you have been thru you are one tough wonderful lady and I love you beyond all means. I would like for you and me to go see

Breaking Away

Sarah together. I want to see for myself how the child is doing. I will be able to help her dollar wise now. Please allow us to do that. I have always felt she was alone without our help. Give this man who loves you, so much, the chance to change his life and live with the most wonderful girl in the world. Please call and let me see you this weekend.

Love, Tom

§

For the next three months, he was more congenial and made an effort to understand where I was coming from. There were no outbursts until the July 4th weekend. My daughter, Terry had ridden up to camp with Tom to spend a few days with us. Because the upstairs of the cabin wasn't finished yet, Tom and I slept in the only bed downstairs and my daughter slept on a pallet just a few feet from us. Tom had not been very interested in sex over the past few years, but on this particular night with the three of us within ten feet of one another, he began to make advances. I was so irritated by his advances I wanted to kick him out of bed. Why now, for heaven's sake? When we could do something, he would ignore me. I punched him a couple

Get Out of My Bed

of times and he finally dozed off, but I think Terry and I got about three hours of sleep between us that night. Between Tom's snoring and Terry's coughing and sneezing, it was impossible to sleep. Tom was up at seven and I got up at eight. I let Terry sleep in because I knew she felt rotten. Besides, this was a break from college and she probably wanted to sleep in. She got up about ten and I started making her some breakfast. She sat on a stool in the middle of the kitchen and we chatted. I had not seen her for a few months. Within a few minutes, Tom walked through the kitchen and gave me one of his "go to hell" looks. I knew I was in trouble. I told Terry to finish her breakfast and I would talk to her when she came outside. In the meantime, Tom called me up to the garage. His face was beet red and I knew I was in for a tongue lashing.

He poked me in the chest with his finger and said, "How dare you fix your daughter's breakfast when you couldn't get out of bed and prepare something for your husband!" I was devastated. He had been so good for the past few months and now everything had gone to hell in a handcart. Whatever progress we had made just flew out the window.

I had reached the breaking point and I started looking for a house to rent in the area. Over a period of

Breaking Away

a few weeks, I searched everywhere but found nothing. During this time, I gave Tom an ultimatum: either he went to a marriage counselor with me or I was leaving. He reluctantly agreed. I located a gentleman only thirty minutes from us, and the first session we each went alone. Tom grumbled about going alone the first time, but I wanted him to talk to this person on a one-to-one basis instead of our getting into a screaming match.

A few days after Tom's first meeting with the counselor, he became more physically aggressive toward me. One night after being in bed about half an hour he jumped up and jerked the covers off me. He started pacing the floor back and forth yelling at me. He kept asking what I was going to tell the counselor about him.

He screamed at me, "Are you going to tell him I've been a good husband and a good provider or are you going to tell him a pack of lies?"

I tried to reason with him and calm him down, but nothing I said mattered. He was in such a mental state that for the first time I really felt physically threatened. I sleep in the nude, so therefore I was curled up in a fetal position trying to stay warm. It was chilly that night and I tried several times to get out of bed to put some clothes on, but he would push me back across the bed. He continued to pace and yell and I became more and more frightened of him.

Finally, he went into the bathroom and I was able to get up and put on some clothes. He came out of the bath and screamed at me for another hour while I sat very meekly in a chair. He finally calmed down and went to bed. For the first time, I began to understand that I might have something more frightening than I had ever imagined, in dealing with Tom. I was now very afraid of what he might do, after seeing him in such a state. I sincerely felt if I had challenged him in any way, or made the situation worse, that I could be hurt badly.

The incident which caused me to leave at any cost happened two weeks later. We had been in bed about an hour when I felt something dripping over my head. I awoke to find Tom pouring a glass of water on me. I asked him if he had totally lost his mind and he only poured more water over my head. He told me to get out of his bed and I replied that I would be more than happy to. I lay on the floor, the remainder of the night, planning how I was going to leave this man.

I knew of a small tenant house which had been vacant for a few years. It was in very bad shape, but I

Breaking Away

had to do something. I contacted the person who owned it, but he wanted me to wait so he could make it more livable. I begged him to let me rent it and explained I needed something immediately. I told him I would do all the painting and cleaning if he would just purchase the paint. He finally agreed.

I planned to move within a week. It would take me a little time to get my belongings packed, which I would have to do when Tom wasn't around. That following weekend would be our last together and I would move out on that Monday. I had made the mistake of confiding in a mutual friend that I was moving out and

33

that weekend we were all at a party together. Tom had found a job about an hour away and was planning on moving to our cabin within the next two weeks. So, I knew it was now or never.

The mutual friend made the comment to Tom, "So you're moving in and Shirley is moving out?" Tom confronted me and I flatly denied that I had any plans to leave. After the few incidents that had recently occurred, there was no way I wanted a confrontation with him. To this day he calls me a liar. Obviously, I would do the same thing again if I had to.

On the night of August 26th, 1986, I moved from our cabin into the little rental house about four or five miles away. The next morning, I had to go out of town to a meeting so I just left all my belongings piled on the floor. Even if I had the time, I couldn't put anything away because everything had to be cleaned and newly painted first. I hired a young man to start painting while I was away. There was no source of heat in the house, so I purchased a wood-burning stove and would have to split my own firewood for the winter. I eventually had two small electric baseboard heaters installed just to keep the pipes from freezing when I was on the road. The little house was only 22 x 29 feet and in need of much repair, but it became my haven. I did not feel totally safe from Tom there, but I wouldn't feel totally safe anywhere. When I returned from the meeting, I was told he was looking for me.

He soon found me at a friend's house and asked if he could please talk to me. He was understandably very upset. Not only had he lost his wife, but he had also lost his job. He had given notice to his previous employer and was moving to camp to take a new position. His new employer had reneged on their offer. He tried to get his previous employer to take him back but they refused.

The following letter was written to me by Tom on that Friday, four days after I left. He obviously did not know he would soon be out of a job.

> Friday night
>
> Dear Shirley,
>
> If you will agree I will live upstairs and not put the stairs in so you can have private quarters. I would only need to use the bath but I will not bother you in any way. We can just live together as friends and I will not sleep with you to give you time to decide if you want to live with me or not. I will help the

Get Out of My Bed

girls and pay as much as I can. I would be happy to be this close to you. I will go to "the doctor" with you and follow his direction. In some way, I must understand what it is I do that upsets you so much. I love you more each day and I want to be with you. We have enough furniture to do for both areas. I pray each hour to let God know how much I love you and for him to touch your heart. There is only one Shirley in the world and I want to show my love to you. I must be stupid in many ways, but I will listen to your words if you will speak from your heart. BJ [our dog] ran away and was gone for hours. I think he looked for you. Come home to us and the snow and the good times. I love you, Shirley, and I will listen to your words. We never gave the "doctor" a chance to help us. I never realized how much love I could have for my angel girl. I will help you with the housework if you want. If you will give this a try and if you are not happy I will move out and leave you to your home here. I built this for you

Breaking Away

and I want you to have it. I do not want to go to my death knowing my Shirley is unhappy. Please let's sit and talk and see if we can work it out to allow you the time and space you want. You are worth any effort I can make to make you happy. My life is short now and I want to spend it with my Shirley. Please come talk to this stupid man who loves you.

I will do my own wash and cleaning--I will eat out also so you can do as you wish. BJ needs you and to have a warm home this winter. I went into shock when you told me you had gone and did not realize that perhaps you were trying to help us by doing it. You can do the same thing here.

I give my word if you tell me how you want it--that is how it will be. Please come back to your home and we can build a happy life for both. If you would help me get started in the new job and you are not happy I will move.

I pray to God that you will come back. We came together by chance and that

Get Out of My Bed

had to have a meaning. Just come for sixty days and if it is not good I will move out. Give me a chance to get back to what I want to be.

Answer my prayer and let's make each other happy. Only death could be worse than losing you. I am proud to have a wife like you. Just come and talk to me.

Tom

§

The second letter, written on Sunday morning at 2 a.m., has a different tone to it:

2:00 a.m.

Sunday

To my wife,

By now you know what has happened, if not, then know they backed out of my job. I talked with the attorney about it and he said I have a positive case. I meet with him on Wed. I find myself with no wife - no job - no car - no money and

Breaking Away

face total loss of everything I (we) have worked for. I will go bankrupt if I cannot get another job fast. I wish this not to happen as we are still married and it will bankrupt you also. The only thing I say is you knew you would leave here as early as Friday and did not say so - you let me quit on Monday knowing full well what you were going to do. I can sue you also and collect damages. I do not want this. I want to resolve our problems and have my Shirley back as she was.

I suggest we do as follows:

- A. I have removed all my things from the lower level of the house.
- B. You come back now and move into the lower level.
- C. I will finish upper part by Sept. 15th. I am being paid until then.
- D. I will bring enough furniture to allow me to live upstairs from the apartment.
- E. We will share the bath - laundry and kitchen.
- F. You have my word under God I will not bother you in any way.

GET OUT OF MY BED

G. I will help you with anything you ask - anytime - any place.

H. This will allow both of us to be ourselves but still know we have a friend to help out if needed.

I. I will take care of the electric and pay what I can if working in any way to help out.

All of this should not have happened if you had talked to me--not everyone else. I would have stayed in Chester--let you live here and we stayed apart until it was over or we went back together. To string me along thinking if I came here we could have worked it out is very unfair. I do not see how you let things on Sunday as they did on our ride when you knew you were leaving.

You told everyone but me. Kate knew at the party but did not tell all.

No human being should be treated this way--but you know what--I still love you. If either or both of us is to live here all of this must be resolved with our friends.

Breaking Away

I ask you in God's name to be just a <u>friend</u> to me now so I can get back on my feet. We both must survive this and I can if you will help.

I do not understand how you could do this. It is now come to an absolute disaster and there was no need for it.

The first issue here is financial <u>survival</u> for both of us. The second issue is how to have a marriage be a good and positive thing for both of us. If the second is not possible then we should <u>help</u> each other to go our separate ways and still be on our feet.

I ask in God's name for you to open your heart and we work together to solve this problem.

Your loving husband, Tom

§

Tom begged me to return home and give him the emotional support he needed since he was now unemployed. I knew that under no circumstances could

Get Out of My Bed

I do this, so I steadfastly refused. When he realized I would not come back as his wife, he started begging me to please spend time with him as a friend. I tried to convince him that a friend relationship wouldn't work either, but he only became more insistent in demanding I spend time with him. I told him that since he had lost his job I would do whatever I could to help him financially, but I was not coming back as his wife.

Chapter 6
Liar, Cheat and Thief

The next few days were filled with many phone calls, arguments, and tears. I stood my ground and insisted I would not come back, but, as usual, trying to reason with Tom got me nowhere. After many battles, I finally gave in and told him I would spend some time with him as a friend. He then asked that if I would spend the night at the cabin, he would sleep upstairs and I would be downstairs and he would leave me alone. I agreed.

The first couple of nights I spent there I was sick with a cold. I welcomed the warmth of our cabin since I had no heat in my little house, but I was also very apprehensive about being under the same roof with Tom. He was on his best behavior those first two nights. He even cooked my dinner, which he had seldom done before. But the situation would not remain calm for very long. I knew it would be my word against Tom's as to who was the sane one here, so I had purchased

Get Out of My Bed

a voice-activated tape recorder and hoped to record one of his outbursts. The opportunity came soon. The following was taken from my diary dated Thursday, September 11, 1986, 8:00 p.m.

From the diary:

> I arrived home from work around six but waited until later to call Tom since I had promised that I would call. I do not want to see him tonight and I'm feeling better after having had a miserable cold. When I called, he said he had my dinner ready and wanted me to come up to see him. I said no, that I was tired and I had already eaten. He began to sound irritated. I tried to make conversation by asking how his day had been and if he had any leads on a job. He would not carry on a conversation with me but hung up. I called him back and asked what happened. He hung up again. I have to stand my ground firmly or what's the use of having left him.

About a half hour had passed since Tom hung up on me. I was in the bathroom and thought I heard a car pull in. I walked to the back door and stepped outside only to see Tom come charging toward me. I backed into the house with him pushing at me and screaming for me to get inside. He was hysterical and I knew if I

Liar, Cheat and Thief

was going to escape this encounter unharmed, I had better stay as cool and calm as possible. He ripped my phone off the wall, threw a pair of snowshoes across the room at me and broke the only chair I had into three pieces. He ranted and raved for over an hour. It was the longest 60 minutes of my life.

He told me he couldn't believe I had moved into such a dump. He said it was just my type of place to live and this is what I deserve. He accused me again of causing him to lose his job and told me he was going to take us both down the tubes. He called me an "F'n nigger" and "whore" and a few other choice names. He said that because I told him I wasn't leaving him and connived and schemed to move, that I was a liar, cheat, and thief. If I had told him I was leaving, I wonder what the outcome would have been.

During this temper tantrum, I remembered that my voice-activated tape recorder was in my purse and ready to go. All I had to do was reach inside and push the appropriate button. I asked Tom if I could get a Kleenex out of my purse and he said okay. The tape recorder was small and Tom had no idea that when I reached for the Kleenex I also activated the recorder. For whatever it's worth, I have part of this nasty violent scene on tape. My attorney knew about the recording but obviously felt it was of no value, for he never asked to use it. I felt that it did prove very abusive behavior since it was my word against Tom's.

He told me I had two choices--to either get out of town or come back to him and he would apologize to all our friends for how I had behaved. He said what he really should do is beat the hell out of me or maybe cut off my hair, which comes to my waist. He said that's what they did during the war. They cut the whore's hair--shaved their heads. Several times during this bizarre scene he grabbed my hair and jerked very hard with me screaming for him to please stop. I tried not to move a muscle or even look at him. I sat cross-legged on the floor while he paced the floor in front of me. Once he used the palm of his hand and hit my forehead, knocking me over. A screen door was within a few feet of me, but it was latched. I knew I wouldn't be able to get out before he caught me if I made a run for it. I also knew that in his present state, if I tried to fight back or get away I could be really hurt.

He continued his screaming and told me he was going to call the company I worked for and tell them exactly what kind of liar and cheat I really am. And when he was finished I would lose my job also. He told me I'm a spoiled brat who has never had anyone tell me I'm wrong. He also thinks I'm very selfish and not capable of loving anyone but myself. That as long as I have my own way everything is fine.

He kept saying I wasn't going to jerk him around anymore. That I have to make up my mind now, either to get a divorce or move back in. He keeps trying to force me into a decision, but in this man's state of mind, I'm not going to tell him I want a divorce.

When I don't agree with him to try to work things out together, you can see the dark clouds form. If I mention anything about getting wood in for the winter or taking anything from our home he gets extremely angry. So how am I supposed to feel safe, by telling him I'm not coming back, and I really want a divorce?

I wish I had someone to turn to for help who could be a mediator between us, but most of our friends don't want to get involved. I really don't want to put our friends in a position of taking sides or listening to our problems. This is my battle and no one else's. I got myself into this and now I have to get myself out. Tom isn't honest with himself about our relationship, so I know he wouldn't be honest with anyone else.

Finally, after throwing a few more verbal daggers at me, Tom began to calm down. He cried and begged me not to leave him. He became relatively sane again and asked that I come up to the house and spend the night. After having lived through the past hour for having refused dinner, I said I would come up, but he had to sleep upstairs. He agreed and the remainder of the evening he was relatively calm and I was the one who was a nervous wreck, but obviously couldn't show it. I had just seen behavior from Tom in which I knew he could become more physical. The situation was becoming more and more complicated.

All I knew was that I wanted to spend as little time in this man's company as possible. But Tom wasn't going to let me get that wish anytime soon. I would just like to have some peace and quiet in my life so that I can relax and gather my thoughts as to how I'm going to solve this problem. One thing I'm certain of is that I have to get Tom out of my life, but that will not be a simple matter.

I was extremely upset that he had lost his job. I had not intended for this problem to be a factor in our separation. I knew it certainly wasn't going to help the situation any, and I just prayed he would find work soon. Tom was in a very unstable emotional state and my chore became that of keeping him calm until he found work and the atmosphere around us became more sane. I had once again seen Tom go into a mad rage and I didn't want that to happen because that rage would always be directed at yours truly.

Tom is still telling me he doesn't understand why I left and doesn't even acknowledge that I've been trying to tell him we have a problem for the past two years. His description of my leaving is that I just one day walked out with no warning. It obviously doesn't count that I tried to get him to see a marriage counselor a year before or that I left for four days the previous April. It's extremely frustrating for the most important person in your life not to listen or understand what you are telling him.

The following letter was written to me by Tom a few hours after his outburst the day before.

Friday

9/12/86

> Words cannot express the sorrow in my heart at this moment. The power of love and the laws of nature cause me to act in a fashion you do not understand. In the wild, animals try to protect their own and fight each other over their mates. The fact that you do not love me as I love you does not put you into the same perspective as I and

you do not want to fight to hold us together. My love for you is so great that when you do things against the bond between us I react in an unacceptable fashion.

I shout at you because you are going against the vows we took and want to destroy the bond between us. As God is my witness I will never harm you in any way. The strange thing about you is that you think you can do as you please and not cause the other person to become upset. When you love you do become upset and you try to fight for your loved ones. Love is a very deep emotional condition that directs the entire function of our lives.

I love you very much and I will forgive and forget all that has happened if you will consider a trial period of being together - working together - playing together - to see if we can find the love the way it was. I spoke with Carl [Tom's brother] tonight. He wants to come down and talk with us. If you need anything at all before Friday call and leave a message. What do you want me to do with BJ [our dog] if I am "gone

Liar, Cheat and Thief

overnight?" Please call so we can talk and I will see you Friday 9:00 a.m.

Love always, Tom

§

That same day. Friday, September 12th, after Tom's outburst on Thursday night, we had an appointment with our marriage counselor. I had insisted that we each have an appointment alone with the doctor. This was our first appointment together.

Tom exhibited very intense anger toward me in front of our counselor. At one point the doctor positioned himself only a couple feet from where we were sitting for fear that Tom was going to physically lash out at me. I think Tom was as angry about having to discuss our problems with this third party as he was angry with me.

He flatly denied ever laying a hand on me. I was astounded he could just flat out lie to this man and never blink an eye. I asked him about his behavior the night before. He stated he had never harmed me and has no intentions of hurting me. The doctor asked Tom to agree not to harm me in any way and he agreed. I sarcastically replied, "Well isn't that just wonderful."

Get Out of My Bed

I knew that nothing Tom said to this man was going to matter to him after he walked out the door. He kept interrupting the conversation, telling the counselor I had maliciously lied to him, referring, of course, to my telling him I wasn't going to leave. He kept saying that if I had just been honest and told him I wanted a divorce, we could have avoided all this turmoil and he wouldn't have lost his job. The very reason I left is the same reason I couldn't tell him. Does that make sense?

To give you some idea of how cunning and insidious he can be in his accusations, I'll give you the following example: During this session with the counselor, Tom turned to me and screamed that I couldn't just come and go on the hill as I pleased. I replied, "Pardon me, would you like to explain what you're talking about?" He replied, "You know exactly what I mean. The way you come and go any time you want. You can't do that!" When you're dealing with someone like Tom you really do begin to think you're losing your mind. He flatly denied he was on the phone day and night begging me to spend time with him. The situation was totally hopeless.

At the end of the meeting with the counselor, Tom turned to me and said. "You are coming up and have dinner with me so we can talk, aren't you? I just

Liar, Cheat and Thief

want to talk to you." I looked at the counselor in total despair. The memory of the night before was fresh in my mind. I said I would, but I would not spend the night. He said okay. I stayed for a few minutes to talk with the doctor after I had made sure Tom was out of the building. The doctor said, "You would like to have dinner with him like I would welcome another $1,000 on my mortgage." I said, "That's for sure." He said that Tom was a very manipulative, controlling man and that I should protect myself and get a good attorney. Obviously, that's easier said than done.

Chapter 7
Patronizing Tom

The next two months were the most miserable of my life. It was a constant battle of emotions. I wanted to stay as far away from Tom as possible and he wanted to chase me down to give it one more try. His mood would be congenial at the beginning of a conversation but when I would refuse to come back to him the dark, moody side to Tom would emerge. I tried to stay away from the subject of whether or not I was coming back but invariably, Tom would back me in a corner and insist on an answer. I knew I wasn't coming back, but I was afraid of telling him.

The memory of his recent rage over my not having dinner with him was enough to make me think twice about discussing separation or divorce at all. He also had started threatening to commit suicide. Therefore, I did whatever I could to keep the peace and at the same time stay out of his way.

Patronizing Tom

When he did insist on my seeing him, I usually went up to the house because I found I could usually slip away from him before the encounter became physically dangerous for me. I knew the signals all too well and patronized him by telling him whatever he wanted to hear, at a particular moment, in order to keep myself safe.

But on a few occasions, I wasn't so lucky. On one particular night, he locked me inside the house and said I could not leave unless I told him what I was going to do. I begged him just to take one day at a time and that I wasn't ready to make a decision. He started pacing back and forth in front of me, lecturing me on how I wouldn't make a commitment to making our relationship work. He worked himself into such anger that he threw a drink in my face and pushed the chair over in which I was sitting. He finally unlocked the door and allowed me to leave. I had bruises on my arm and backside for the next few days.

I never teased or instigated an argument with Tom. I would have definitely found myself in a very dangerous position. The situation was very volatile and I was not interested in anything but getting through this problem as emotionally and physically safe as possible. I did not want any harm to come to

Get Out of My Bed

Tom either. I simply knew I could not spend another day in my life as this man's wife.

But no matter how I tried to keep the atmosphere calm, there were still several intense encounters with Tom during those crazy months. On the weekend of September 20th, he called to tell me I had some packages that UPS had left for me. Obviously, this was bait to get me up there. I knew that he wouldn't drop them off for me. I told him I would stop by Sunday afternoon to pick them up. On Sunday about 3:30 he called to ask when I would be there. I went up about 5:30 and knew the moment I arrived that I had to get the packages and leave as soon as possible. Tom was very irritable and asked me to have dinner with him. I said no, that I had already eaten and that I needed to get back home to finish more paperwork. He told me I wasn't going to jerk him around anymore and that I was going to tell him what my plans are. I was terrified to tell him I wanted a divorce and I knew in my gut that he was in no state of mind to hear those words. I tried to talk to him calmly and at the same time back out the door. I started running for my car and he caught me just as I opened the door. He grabbed my shoulder and my hair and literally dragged me back in the house. I screamed so loud and so long I can't believe no one heard me. He threw me across the living room and told me I would

Patronizing Tom

have dinner with him. I agreed but asked that we eat outside because I felt safer there.

As we were eating a friend of ours who was helping Tom with carpentry work stopped to chat. I have never been so happy to see anyone in my life. As he was walking down the drive I met him and told him not to leave unless I was gone also. After we finished the meal I picked up my packages and left without a word to either of them. Tom left his friend sitting at the table, for he immediately followed me home and sat in my drive for what seemed like hours begging me to come back. I stood beside his car and listened to him because I was afraid to go into the house. I felt more comfortable in the open where I could make a run for it if I had to. I knew I was in better physical shape than Tom was.

This letter was written to me two days after the encounter.

Tue Sept 23, 1986

Dear Shirley.

I have had hours and hours to reflect upon many things. One of those things is how when I love you so much is how I have hurt you so much. For the last many years,

Get Out of My Bed

I have been in a position to be the boss. I now feel I could not separate work from personal life. I can now and I am not the boss anymore.

I think the original quest that brought us together still exists in our hearts. I think that God is love. I see the love you have for the creatures on earth and I see love. I see a deep-rooted sense of feeling for all things in you which prior to now did not exist within me. I crashed thru as I pleased thinking I was strong and could do as I wished.

This understanding I now have shows me how wrong I have been in many ways. I think you could class me as a bigot.

The spirit of love and the driving force of God to understand all things in their proper place has finally reached me. BJ [our dog] is a true example of total love.

So many things have been wrong in my life. My feeling about black people is wrong.

God has touched me by showing me that we must live by love and that you have been right. I have been wrong.

Patronizing Tom

My abuse of you is a prime example of my thinking that I can do by strength what can only be done by love.

You have my oath under God that love will guide my life from now on. The old Tom is gone. The winter will be cold and dark but can be warm and full of light if we join our hearts in love and live in peace and joy and quiet. I am ready to go to work soon and I <u>will</u> make it.

I ask you to come so we can talk together and let love guide us to a good life. I understand how hard this must have been for you as my direction has been so bad.

Believe in what I say and allow me to prove to you that my life is changed. Please come so we can talk. I love to sit and talk with you so more of your goodness will rub off.

Love,

Your husband, Tom

Get Out of My Bed

§

In the next few weeks, Tom began to use a new approach by telling me he was going to a lawyer and file for divorce. I hoped that he would but knew that it would not happen. He told me I had no grounds for divorce but that he did. He said he could file because I had abandoned him and because of mental cruelty. I don't know of another human being who is more pompous than Tom. I begged him for two years to see a counselor and tried every trick in the book to hold our marriage together and now he's telling me he's going to file for divorce on the grounds of mental cruelty. I didn't know whether to laugh or cry.

During one of the nights I spent with him, he came downstairs and knelt by my bed. He had promised he wouldn't bother me but said he just wanted to talk. I asked him to please leave me alone. After professing his love for me several times he started pushing to have sex. I flatly refused. He became very indignant and said he could file for divorce on grounds of my refusing him sexually. I told him to stick it in his ear. He told me I was a rotten, selfish bitch, and that he doesn't understand why I'm so bitter towards him. If he doesn't understand by now, then he obviously never will. He proceeded to tell me I must be going through the change. The only change I needed was to get this man out of my life.

Patronizing Tom

Even when Tom would stay upstairs as he had promised, he would be screaming down to me to get that dog out of my bed. He knew I would probably let BJ sleep at the foot of my bed. It was like Tom was possessed to control whatever he could in my life no matter how minor or major.

Chapter 8
Keeping the Peace

  In October I became aware of a book titled <u>Men Who Hate Women and the Women Who Love Them</u> by Dr. Susan Forward. It had been published in September and gave me great strength in dealing with Tom. Dr. Forward describes the type of personality who becomes abusive and gives you several ways to deal with this destructive relationship. As I read the book I was amazed at the similarities in Tom's personality to those cases Dr. Forward had counseled. This is a wonderful self-help guide for rebuilding your self-esteem and helping your mate change and get back to a loving, mutually acceptable relationship. But if your spouse refuses to listen to your suggestions or those of a professional counselor then you have no choice but to separate yourself from this person. If you stay in an abusive relationship, your self-esteem and worthiness will be destroyed. You are the guardian of your own soul and self-respect, and you have to take

Keeping the Peace

this responsibility or you will live a miserable life. The first two weeks of October were fairly calm until Tom gave me an ultimatum of either moving back in as a "friend" or else going down the tubes financially. He said if I didn't move back he would have no inspiration to work or pay the bills. Again, he stated he would live upstairs and I could have the downstairs except for sharing the kitchen and bath. What a choice.

Tom gave me this ultimatum over the weekend of the 11th and stated that he wanted me to have dinner with him the following Tuesday and give him my answer. I was unable to have dinner with him that night but went up to see him that Wednesday. I had been a nervous wreck for the past few days because I knew there was no way I could move back in and when I told him no, I didn't know what his reaction would be. But when I saw him that night he never brought up the subject. I had dinner with Dr. Jekyll. He had prepared our meal and was very congenial. He told me he knew he had been 900% wrong and that I had to be a free spirit in order to decide what I wanted. I couldn't believe what I was hearing. I actually thought that maybe he was understanding what our problems were and he might come to his senses. He allowed me to leave after dinner with no argument and was a perfect gentleman.

Get Out of My Bed

I should have known it was too good to be true, for I saw him on Friday night and he was in a very bad mood. Mr. Hyde was back. He asked me why I didn't give him an answer on Wednesday regarding moving back in. I replied that the subject never came up. He told me I was avoiding the issue. He went into one of his tirades and I got the whole nine-yard lecture on how he was willing to make a commitment and all I would give was a big fat zero.

I told him I would do whatever I could to help him but I would not move back in. I told him I would be his friend, help work in the house, help financially if I could, but I would not move back in. I knew the tension was mounting to the point that I was not going to be safe much longer so I made a run for the car and fortunately was able to get away from him. But I knew in my gut that he might follow so instead of going home, I pulled in behind a barn next to my house and turned off the car lights. Tom had followed me and pulled in and out of my drive looking for me. I sat there for at least an hour trying to decide what to do. I had already spent several nights with friends so that Tom couldn't find me, but I didn't want to bother anyone. I just wanted to be home in my own bed. I decided to leave my car behind the barn, sneak into

Keeping the Peace

the house and leave the lights on as they were. I hoped Tom would think I wasn't there and I would be safe. I safely got into the house and crawled into bed with a flashlight and the book, "Men Who Hate Women and the Women Who Love Them." Things were quiet and I read for about a half hour. The phone rang several times but I, of course, did not answer.

I then heard what I thought was a car pull in and out of my drive but then I heard someone at my back door. A pane of glass had been replaced with a piece of plexiglass and Tom was able to push it out, reach in, and unlock the door. I could not believe what I was hearing. This man was actually breaking into my house. I was so petrified that I actually froze in my bed. I think I even tried not to breathe. Tom had a flashlight and came walking through the house calling my name.

He came into the bedroom and knelt beside my bed and asked why I was playing games and wanted to know where my car was. He stayed there for about a half hour professing his love for me, begging me to come back and stating he knew we could work things out. I have never felt so vulnerable or unsafe in my life. He had previously asked to take me on a date to hear the orchestra in a nearby city. He asked if I would go with him the next night. I told him I would go if he

Get Out of My Bed

would please leave. He finally left but only if I promised that I would go with him the next night. When he was gone, I became totally hysterical. I screamed and cried and tried to think of someone I could call and talk to. I tried to call a friend but she wasn't home. And then I thought what better person to call than Tom. There are no words to describe how humiliated and angry I felt. So, I called Tom and screamed at him that if he "ever did such a thing again I would see that his ass rotted in jail." He told me very calmly just to settle down, that everything was okay.

The next evening, I kept my promise and went with Tom to hear the orchestra. It was one of the hardest things I have ever done in my life. Trying to make conversation was next to impossible.

He, again, was a perfect gentleman and all I wanted to do was throw up. In other words, that night I was with Dr. Jekyll, but I knew Mr. Hyde was somewhere in the shadows.

In the next few weeks, he again told me he was going to file for divorce and my reply was, "Please do." But I later received the following letter dated Oct. 22, 1986.

Keeping the Peace

Dear Shirley,

I love you too much and I could not do it. There must be a way for us to work this out. If you would spend Sat and Sunday only with me I would be very happy for that. I would like to do something with you on Sat eve. I had a good time and we did not fuss.

I get upset because you don't seem to care about all the good things. The good things were much more than the bad. Your hard work here with the flowers and with the house will all be wasted if we part. Your rabbits will die without us to look after them. BJ will not be looked after right.

If you would just say something to me as to what you want and how you feel I can understand.

If you want to be alone for a month I can live with that. I can live with anything which gives us hope. Please open your heart to me. Tell me what it is. Why are you so uncaring? Please promise me to call and talk to me on the phone. I cannot give up. I love you more than ever now. You are trying in some way to make me understand something I do not now understand. I know

Get Out of My Bed

that if someone hurts you it is hard to forgive. The difference is if they hurt you on purpose. I did not hurt you on purpose. I do not want to control you. You are a free spirit and I love you for it. Please call me so we can talk. Shirley was my joy, my love - my idol - Shirley was all the good things in life to me. She was what I <u>always</u> wanted to be. She showed me the good life in the woods.

Let's not throw all this away! I promise you under God that if we try <u>you can live exactly as you want to live</u> and show me a better life at the same time. Dear beautiful Shirley please - let's talk on the phone. You talk, I will listen. We must resolve this so we can see the sunshine - smell the flowers - enjoy each day. Your letter said you never felt more loved. It is true and that love is forever!

Love, Tom

§

The letter Tom refers to stating that I never felt more loved was written during our first month of marriage.

Chapter 9
Unsafe Desperation

Tom became more desperate in his fight to get me back. His threats and harassment ranged from promises of rewards for returning, to threats of financial ruin if I didn't. He informed me that I was over-the-hill and that no other man would want me anyway. He told me that if we didn't file our income taxes together for the 1986 year I was going to have to pay $2000 in income tax. He once told me that if I came back he would buy me a horse or a new snowmobile.

Of course, the biggest guilt trip was that if I didn't return and he had to file bankruptcy it would be my fault. And in the same breath, he would say that if I didn't come back he wouldn't have the motivation to work. He had found work and I was hoping he was getting back on his feet. But what Tom told me and what was the truth was usually very different.

Tom was never able or willing to discuss why I had left to begin with or come to grips with his behavior to-

Get Out of My Bed

ward me and make a concerted effort in understanding how I felt. I gave him every opportunity possible not only to help save our marriage but to help Tom look into his own personality and try to understand why he treats his loved ones the way he does. After we saw a marriage counselor together twice, he did not want to go to a session again. His excuse was that he wasn't getting anything out of it and that no one else could solve our problems. If a person does not freely go for counseling there is no way he is going to acknowledge the reason for being there in the first place. I could only lead him in that direction but Tom simply refused to see the counselor again. I begged him to go but there was no hope.

After he had seen the counselor for the first time alone, I asked Tom what he thought of the person and if he was able to speak freely to him. Tom replied that the counselor said that I was taking advantage of him. I started laughing and told Tom that there was no way he would have said such a thing since I have never even met him. Tom became very angry and asked if I was calling him a liar. I replied that no counselor worth his weight in salt would say such a thing on the first visit. I could see Tom becoming very agitated, so I dropped the subject.

Unsafe Desperation

When I went to see the doctor myself, I laughed and told him what Tom had said. He told me he may have asked Tom that type of question but certainly did not say I was taking advantage of Tom. I knew that was the case. After speaking with the counselor for a while he replied that my side of the story was totally different from my husband's. I said that I didn't really care what Tom had told him because this was the truth and my reality and that I could not deal with it anymore. He replied that if what I was telling him was the truth he could certainly understand why I needed help.

I knew from Tom's first session that it was unlikely he would speak truthfully and openly with this third party. But anything was worth a try. I continued to go for counseling alone. I needed an educated stranger to tell me that I was not the person who was out to lunch here. I was desperate to find answers to help me solve this insane situation.

I knew I would be filing for divorce soon but was still trying to keep myself safe and convince Tom I wanted a legal separation. So far, I was afraid to say I wanted a divorce.

October became November and hunting season opened, for which I was very grateful. For the past few years, Tom's brother and brother-in-law had come to

Get Out of My Bed

hunt and that meant Tom would have company and would not be harassing me about spending time with him. So, things were fairly peaceful for me during that week before Thanksgiving. But he started begging me to spend the Thanksgiving holiday with him. I knew that my daughter would be coming to visit from college and he would not touch me if she were with us. So, I agreed that she and I would spend Wednesday and Thursday nights with him and then on Friday I would drive her back to school. Things were tense during Thanksgiving, but we got through it. But when I was ready to leave, Tom made a comment about purchasing a new snowmobile that day. I didn't say a word, but I was furious. He had been complaining about money and then proceeded to tell me he was considering buying a new sled. Not to mention the fact that I gave him permission to cash in the $3200 of stock that I had earned which was being held as collateral for the Creek Road property. He paid off the $2000 note on the property, and I told him to keep the remaining $1200 to help with bills he had incurred while out of work.

That Friday I drove my daughter back to school and returned to my little house. I made no contact with Tom and hoped that he would not bother me. On Sunday morning he called at 8:30. He was very upset and said that the commode had run half the night and flooded

Unsafe Desperation

the downstairs. He asked if I could come up and help him move the rug and furniture. So, I went up to help him. I was still angry over his comment about looking at new sleds and I told him so, especially since he had been threatening bankruptcy. I should have known I couldn't raise my voice to him. He replied that he wasn't going to get a new sled until his commission check came in. I said that I could not believe that under the circumstances he was even considering such a thing.

He became very angry and shoved me into a chair beside the kitchen counter, He asked me what I was planning on doing about our relationship and I said I wanted a divorce. Wrong thing to do! He started choking me and banged my head against the kitchen counter. I told him to give me two weeks and then I would give him my answer. The largest butcher knife in the house happened to be lying on the counter within his reach. He picked it up and held it beside my head and asked again what I was going to do. I obviously told him we would work things out. He seemed to calm down and soon allowed me to leave.

He called me later that day and said he was going to see an attorney and file for divorce. He said that he would be gone for a few days and that he was taking our dog with him. He knew that would upset me. I yelled at

Get Out of My Bed

him about his outburst that morning and he told me he could have me shot. Then he said he could shoot me and then kill himself. I said that would certainly solve everything. He told me I was no longer welcome on the hill since I had been treating him the way I had. Does he not understand that's the last place I want to be anyway?

Chapter 10
Divorce - Another Story

Towards the end of July, I had met with an attorney and sought advice regarding a divorce. At that time, he informed me that since I had been a resident of the state less than a year I could not file. This information was very depressing and I had resolved myself to staying with Tom until I could file. Toward the end of September, I sought legal counsel again, from another attorney. He informed me I could file for divorce because Tom had become physically abusive. I explained to him that Tom was threatening me with bankruptcy and stating he was going to take me down the proverbial tubes. I asked if I was responsible for Tom's personal debt. His answer was no, but he did not go into detail to explain to me what the laws were regarding finances.

I may have separated myself physically from Tom by moving out, but my getting a divorce would also become a monumental struggle.

GET OUT OF MY BED

On December 10th Tom was served with both divorce papers and an order of protection. This seemed to have a sobering effect on him, but I knew that Mr. Hyde was always lurking somewhere in this man's personality. Basically, the one thing the order of protection did was to keep him away from me, which was a tremendous relief.

The action for divorce and order of protection read as follows:

>ACTION FOR DIVORCE
>
>AFFIDAVIT

Now come Shirley Snow and after first being duly sworn deposed and says that:

1. I am the plaintiff in this action and am making this Affidavit in supplement to my financial affidavit which is attached hereto and made a part hereof and in support of my application of this Court to issue · Orders against the defendant against harassing me and alienating any of our marital assets prior to the conclusion of this litigation.

Divorce - Another Story

2. I was married to the defendant on November 25, 1979, in Harrisville, Pennsylvania. I separated from the defendant in August of 1986. The actions of the defendant which gave rise to this suit occurred in the state of Pennsylvania.

3. Despite our separation, the defendant has continued his long-standing pattern of perpetrating violence against me. On November 30, 1986, at approximately 8:30 A.M. while I was meeting with the defendant to discuss our difficulties, he abruptly went into a rage, began choking me, banging my head on a wood counter, and drawing a large butcher knife out against me and threatening to kill me.

4. The defendant has also threatened to alienate our marital assets prior to the completion of these proceedings so as to deny me my rightful share of our assets.

WHEREFORE, your deponent prays that this Court grant unto me a Protective Order and an Order restraining the defendant from alienating any of our assets.

Get Out of My Bed

§

ACTION FOR DIVORCE

ORDER TO SHOW CAUSE

LET THE DEFENDANT (Tom Snow) SHOW CAUSE upon the Affidavit of the Plaintiff dated December 8, 1986 and all the proceedings heretofore had herein, why a Protective Order should not be issued against the defendant as well as a restraining order against alienating any assets of the marriage during the pendency of this suit as well as why such other and further relief as to the Court may seem just and proper should not be granted. The defendant may show such cause at a Regular Term of this Court to be held at the Court House on December 15, 1986, beginning at 9:30 A.M. or as soon thereafter as counsel and the parties can be heard by this Court. At such time, the defendant may appear personally or through counsel and present his arguments, either orally or in writing,

Divorce - Another Story

as to why the aforesaid relief should not be granted.

It appearing to the satisfaction of this Court that such service is possible and proper, personal service of a copy of this Order and its accompanying papers as aforesaid upon the defendant on or by December 11, 1986, shall be deemed good and sufficient service.

§

It was not until after my divorce that I discovered my attorney had allowed a mutual order of protection. He never told me this and he never gave me the order to carry with me which I should have had. I was never served with any papers; therefore, I never knew the order was mutual until I requested a copy of the papers served on Tom several months later. W h e n you are ignorant of the system you find these things out after the fact. The order of protection reads as follows:

Get Out of My Bed

ACTION FOR
DIVORCE

ORDER

This matter having come on for a Motion for temporary relief in this divorce proceeding and after reviewing the affidavit of the plaintiff dated December 8, 1986, as well as the Stipulating Letter of the Attorney for the Defendant, Allen Walker, Esq., dated December 10, 1986 and after hearing arguments in favor of the said motion from Dick Jackson, Esq., Attorney for the Plaintiff and due deliberation having been had hereon

NOW, upon motion of Dick Jackson, Esq., Attorney for the Plaintiff, it is

ORDERED, ADJUDGED, AND DECREED, that a mutual protective order is hereby granted wherein the parties are enjoined and directed not to frighten, harass, bother, assault, annoy, or otherwise embarrass the other which such directive shall be known as a joint protective order, and it is further

Divorce - Another Story

ORDERED, ADJUDGED AND DECREED, that neither party shall not transfer or otherwise assign any interest they may have in marital property, pending further Order of this Court.

§

I was furious when I discovered it was a mutual order and I wrote to the judge who issued the order. I described to the judge some of the abuse I had endured and told him it was a further humiliation that he should grant a mutual order of protection. If anything, physical did occur again between us, it would be my word against his.

I explained that I attended a meeting in a large neighboring city regarding domestic violence in which these same issues were discussed among abused women, law enforcement, judges, counselors, etc. This meeting was held by the state coalition against domestic violence and one of the goals was to find ways to improve the legal system. The two judges attending the meeting stated that they never issue mutual orders of protection. It is my opinion that not only is a mutual order worthless, but an insult to the person being abused.

GET OUT OF MY BED

I received the following reply from the judge:

Dear Mrs. Snow:

I am in receipt of your letter of December 5, 1988. <u>Section 100.3 (a) of the Rules Governing Judicial Conduct</u> states in part that a judge, "except as authorized by law, (shall) neither initiate nor consider <u>exparte</u> or other communications concerning a pending or impending matter."

I do not grant mutual orders of protection without the consent of both parties or their respective counsel, which was, obviously, the case in this matter. The further questions raised in your letter should be addressed to your attorney. I am forwarding a copy of your letter to your attorney as well as to counsel for Mr. Snow.

Very truly yours,

§

If you find it necessary to have a protective order served on your spouse or boyfriend, make sure it is issued only for you and carry the order on your per-

Divorce - Another Story

son at all times. If an encounter occurs and you have the proof with you, the police officer can immediately throw the person in jail. If not, it is your word against his.

A week after I served Tom with the divorce papers he called and I knew it was Dr. Jekyll speaking. He started the conversation by telling me how much he loved me and, "couldn't we work things out. Can't we at least try for a while?" He said he was a different person but I wouldn't give him a chance to prove it. He said he was lonely and needed me and that we could have a wonderful life together. When I replied that I was not interested, I could hear Mr. Hyde enter the conversation. He asked, "Are you happy there alone? Don't you need anyone? There must be something wrong with you, Shirley since you failed at this marriage too. You're a loser."

He told me that if I would sign over the property he would pay all of our debts. I said that I would not and he got nastier. He told me he had heard rumors about me and that people in town were talking about me. I said, "Oh, really - like what?" He replied that he had heard that I was a lesbian.

I said, "Oh, really?" He said I should leave town for my own sake. I finally just hung up on him. He would spread any lies he could about me just to protect

Get Out of My Bed

his male ego. If I have to explain or defend myself to anyone who has known me for any length of time then they obviously are not my friends anyway.

Tom called again on December 20th at 12:30 a.m. I told him I wouldn't talk at that hour and that he shouldn't bother me again. He called the next morning and told me he wasn't feeling well.

He told me he loved me and wanted me back. I said no and he changed his tune. He started talking about my signing everything over to him again and I said that I would not. I called him a bastard and hung up. He called back and told me it wasn't "ladylike" to call him names.

In January I received a bill for my daughter's car insurance which had been due on the 15th of December. It had been canceled because of lack of payment. The bill had been mailed to Tom and he very conveniently didn't send it to me until it had been canceled. No matter how much I explained the situation to the insurance company they couldn't care less. It cost me an hour of long distance phone calls and a higher rate for the insurance. The bill was due December 15th and I received it from Tom on the 15th of January. Tom addressed the envelope to Shirley with no last name. I had an appointment with our marriage counselor and explained to him some of the problems I was having.

Divorce - Another Story

He told me this was Tom's way of trying to frustrate me. And the more he frustrated me, the weaker I would become and maybe he would get me back. The counselor said it was a very calculated way of trying to pull me down and that I could not allow him to do this.

In February I received the following note from Tom:

Feb 87

To Shirley,

I now understand why you did what you had to do. The job and my boss were killing me and then I drank too much which made me irrational. I am the old Tom now. Please give me just a chance to prove this to you. I will follow your lead to a good life for both of us. I love you and want to make up for all this heartache. Let's talk and do things together for a while so I can show you how good a husband I can be to you. Talk to me - show me, fuss at me I will understand. Let's work together and bring all the good things back.

Please call or write and let's live and love on the hill.

Love,

Get Out of My Bed

§

Towards the end of February on a snowy Sunday morning, Tom called at 2 a.m. and then again at 8 a.m. It was Dr. Jekyll calling and he told me that a friend of ours was there snowmobiling and wanted to see me. He said that if I wanted to come up and go for a ride he would send our friend down to get me and he promised not to argue about anything. He also said that if I came up I could take my sled back home. I very hesitatingly agreed and asked that our friend come down to get me. I had really missed my snowmobile and I wanted it in a bad way. So, I took the bait, but it was the old "dangle the carrot" routine. He had no intention of letting me have the snowmobile.

When we got to the cabin I informed our friend not to leave me alone with Tom under any circumstances. Our friend informed me that Tom wanted to go with me alone and I said absolutely not. So the three of us went for a ride for a couple hours. We stopped at a local watering hole and during this time the bribery started. Once more he said he would buy me a horse or a new snowmobile if I would come back. Our friend finally told him to knock it off.

When we returned to the cabin I said I was going

Divorce - Another Story

home now and that I would take my sled. He had accomplished what he wanted which was getting me up to the cabin. So now, what he had promised a few hours earlier was totally irrelevant. He said he really preferred that I left it because it needed a lot of work and he would get it fixed for me. At that point, I was kicking myself in the rear end because I should have known better. I wasn't about to argue with him. So, I went home empty handed.

Chapter 11
Out of Control

One of the most overwhelming feelings during my marriage was that I was losing any kind of <u>control over my own existence and destiny</u>. I felt that I had no say in any facet of our relationship. I felt that my opinion to this person meant nothing. If Tom had ever asked my opinion or I gave it anyway, on any subject, he did what he wanted to. For example, before I moved out, I had to leave for a few days on a business trip. When I returned, two of our friends were in the process of installing paneling in the cabin.

I was never asked if I even wanted paneling or if I liked that particular color. I eventually developed a "why bother" attitude. More and more I just didn't talk, because it didn't matter what I said anyway.

I certainly would not be able to regain any self-esteem or feeling of being a worthwhile human being by allowing Tom's psychological battering to continue.

OUT OF CONTROL

My only defense left was to leave. I was desperate to regain some control over my own well-being and destiny.

But if I felt that I had no control over any part of my life when I was married to Tom, I definitely felt out of control when two attorneys became involved in this hopeless situation. I was told by my attorney that Tom's legal counsel refused to return phone calls and that Tom was fighting the divorce. I knew Tom was fighting the divorce, but his attorney not returning phone calls was a flat out lie.

In January my attorney received a reply from Tom regarding my divorce action. Basically, it stated that if I would sign everything over he would pay all of our so-called debts.

In the middle of March, I received the following correspondence from my attorney. Tom's bank account and other finances were still based in Pennsylvania which I was told made matters more difficult.

Dear Shirley:

Mr. Snow seems always to be in Pennsylvania. I therefore will appreciate your contacting me to discuss procedures to

Get Out of My Bed

remove your belongings from the subject premises.

Naturally. I shall keep you advised of the other developments in this matter.

§

At the end of April, I received a letter from Jackson stating that Tom and I, and the two attorneys could meet in his office at 1 p.m. on May 22nd to give our depositions regarding our finances. A court reporter was present and recorded both our testimonies. A deposition gives both attorneys the opportunity to ask either spouse whatever questions they choose regarding the divorce case. I don't believe Jackson did anything with any of the information that he obtained that day. But he did make $340.00 for the four hours we were there.

On May 11th I checked my phone messages and a lady from the Master Charge department of Society Bank stated that it was urgent that I call her. This charge card was issued in both names but was used primarily by Tom.

I called Tom and asked him why this woman was calling me. He replied that since I had not signed any papers it was out of his hands. Tom had always

OUT OF CONTROL

made the payments on this card but had given her my number to call just to harass me. Now he is resorting to blackmail.

During the conversation, he said that he had been in the hospital and now owed over $6,000.00 in medical bills. Tom had always suffered from high blood pressure and we had a medicine cabinet full of prescriptions which he usually refused to take.

He had also blamed me for having no medical insurance. During the time span from August 26th to December 10th, he had been on my medical plan through my employer which provided good coverage. But when I filed for legal separation that coverage became void. He always accused me of calling the company and having him deleted from the plan, but medical insurance at that time was the last thing on my mind. He knew the 800 number to call my company to inquire about continuing coverage for a monthly charge but he never called to my knowledge. I later learned there was a plan available for this type of situation.

Tom's attorney once told a friend of mine that I could be held responsible for Tom's medical bills. This may be true in some situations, but the issue was never pressed. Should I be responsible for arranging medical

Get Out of My Bed

insurance for a man who is threatening to kill me?

By June I was extremely frustrated because the lines of communication seemed to be nonexistent. Getting this man out of my life was becoming a monumental task and no one seemed to be able to help me. I started trying to think of a way I could get something accomplished. So I proposed the following to my attorney:

> PLEASE TAKE NOTICE, that upon the annexed Affidavits of Shirley Snow as Plaintiff, being duly sworn on the 19th day of June, 1987 and upon all the proceedings heretofore had herein, a motion will be made of this Court to be held at the Supreme Court Chambers, Second Floor County Office Building, on the 6th day of July, 1987, beginning at 9:30 A.M. granting to the plaintiff the following relief to wit:
>
> A. Exclusive possession of the marital premises on Creek Road.
>
> B. Return of all personal items to plaintiff.
>
> C. For such other and further relief as to the court may seem just and proper.

Out of Control

PLEASE TAKE FURTHER NOTICE, that answering affidavits in this matter must be presented to the undersigned within five (5) days of the return date of this Motion.

Shirley Snow, being duly sworn, deposes and says that:

1. That she is the plaintiff in the above-entitled action and that she is currently residing at Box 69, Cold Springs.

2. That she makes this affidavit in support of her Motion to direct defendant to release plaintiff's personal items from marital premises; for exclusive possession of the marital premises located on Creek Road, Cold Springs, and for such other and further relief as to the Court may seem just and proper.

3. Arrangements had been made for plaintiff to remove her personal items from the premises on June 13, 1989 at 12:00 P.M., of which defendant relinquished.

Get Out of My Bed

4. That ever since the separation of the parties hereto, on or about August of 1986, plaintiff has been forced to rent premises and defendant has had exclusive possession, unjustly of both marital premises of Creek Road, Cold Springs, and 1849 Maple Lane, Harrisville. Plaintiff has been forced to reside at other premises, of which she had to rent as she was fearful of her life. Defendant has on numerous occasions pulled plaintiff's hair, threatened to kill plaintiff and has choked plaintiff. These acts of violence against plaintiff, therefore cause plaintiff to rent premises other than the marital premises, of which defendant had access to.

5. That there is currently a note outstanding of approximately Five Thousand Dollars ($5,000.00) for the property commonly known as 1849 Maple Lane, Harrisville.

6. That the plaintiff will pay note due for approximately Five Thousand Dollars ($5,000.00) on 1849 Maple Lane, Har-

Out of Control

risville properties and have exclusive possession of Creek Road, Cold Springs; return of personal merchandise; plaintiff will have ability to deduct One-Half (1/2) percent interest on income tax; with the court to determine a final equitable distribution of assets at time of trial taking this and all of the factors into consideration.

WHEREFORE, your deponent prays that this motion be granted allowing plaintiff exclusive possession of the marital premises commonly known as Creek Road, Cold Springs; that the plaintiff pay note due on 1849 Maple Lane, Harrisville, properties in the amount of approximately Five Thousand Dollars ($5,000.00) and that plaintiff be granted the ability to deduct One-Half (1/2) interest on income tax; that all personalities be returned to her by defendant; and for such other and further relief as to the court may seem just and proper.

Get Out of My Bed

§

The following was Tom's reply:

Tom Snow, being duly sworn, does hereby depose and say that:

1. I am the defendant in the above entitled action and make this Answering Affidavit in response to plaintiff's motion and affidavit of June 19, 1987.

2. I wholeheartedly agree that the plaintiff be allowed to pay the $5,000 pursuant to our joint note of September 15, 1984 for $20,000. I agree that if my wife pays such amount, she be entitled to deduct one-half of the interest payments from her income tax return.

3. I agree that my wife may have the return of the personal property which I have already packed for her at the former marital residence.

4. I was present at said premises on June 13, 1987 at approximately 12:00 p.m. My wife never arrived.

At approximately noon on such date, I contacted my wife by phone and asked

OUT OF CONTROL

her when she was planning to pick up the personality. She advised that she could not locate help to assist her. I suggested that I would assist her and would contact a mutual friend to assist us.

My wife refused and stated that she would take care of these matters later.

Until receipt of this motion, I have received no further request from my wife to pick up the personality.

5. My wife abandoned me and the marital premises on August 26, 1986 and has not returned to date.

   My wife is welcome to resume residence with me at any time. The allegations of plaintiff's paragraph number "4" are completely false and perjurious. At no time did I ever present any threat to her well-being.

6. My wife has acknowledged her agreement to a lease of the 1849 Maple Lane property to Dan Smith. Such lease, with option to purchase, as dated February 25, 1986. The lease is for the term of four years beginning March, 1990. Mr. Smith

remains current in his payments and, therefore, cannot be terminated.

For my wife to suggest that this property is within my exclusive possession is totally false.

In fact, the financial shortfall on the Harrisville property is costing me in excess of $700.00 per month (approximately $300.00 per month on first mortgage; approximately $400.00 on second mortgage).

7. My wife earns approximately $32,000.00 a year in a very stable job position. Pursuant to her financial affidavit of December 4, 1986, she pays $125.00 per month rent on her premises. This case was sued back in early December, 1986, some seven months ago. A financial examination before trial was held on May 22, 1987. Obviously, there are other motives herein involved than those disclosed in plaintiff's motion papers.

8. My attorney advises that he was not even contacted as concerns the relief herein requested.

Out of Control

I am forced to expend substantial sums of money to defend this motion which has no validity.

I have been forced to take a very substantial decrease in pay and am barely able to avoid bankruptcy.

My wife is in a much superior financial situation and should not be permitted to take advantage of same by forcing me to expend substantial money to defend her spurious motions.

Therefore, I am asking the Court to grant me $500.00 in attorney's fees for the defense of this motion.

§

We had a court date to present this motion to the judge but my attorney decided not to do so. When I questioned him as to why he did not present the motion, he stated that he was afraid he would lose and he didn't want to do that at this time. The only thing I accomplished was a date to pick up some of my belongings from the cabin. Jackson also advised me to pay $2,500.00, which was half the note due.

Get Out of My Bed

He stated that I should do so to show good faith. I paid the $2,500.00 in September of 1987. This was a $5,000.00 second mortgage note which was due on our Harrisville home. I'm not sure who was recipient of the so-called good faith.

We had leased the Harrisville property with an option to purchase to a Dan Smith and his family. At the time, the agreement appeared to be working well.

But there was one slight flaw in the agreement Tom had made with Dan Smith. Since my name was also on the mortgage, the agreement wasn't worth a nickel since Tom did not have me sign it. Mr. Smith later told me that my not signing these papers was a factor among many others which made him decide not to purchase the home. It wasn't that I refused to sign their agreement, I simply was never asked by Tom to do so.

Finally, a court date was set for November 10th, but much to my dismay the Judge became ill and it was postponed to December 17th.

On December 4, 1987 the following letter was written by Tom's doctor:

OUT OF CONTROL

RE: TOM SNOW

To Whom it may concern:

Mr. Snow was recently hospitalized with the diagnosis of Malignant Hypertension and Angina Pectoris.

Since his work-up found that his hypertension was in a big part due to his stressful personal and business problems, we have advised him to have no contact via lawyer or court system for the next three months, or until we can get his blood pressure under control.

He also will be in counseling for better ways to handle stress. He is currently taking medications that could possibly make him more symptomatic until the side-effects abate.

Please excuse him from any court appearances or briefing on current marital status for the next three months.

§

I called the hospital where Tom's physician practices and Tom had been admitted on November 27th and

GET OUT OF MY BED

released December 3rd. The 4th was a Friday. Tom was seen snowmobiling that weekend and he flew to Portugal on business the following week.

I wrote the following letter to the State Medical Board:

To Whom it May Concern
December 28th

I would like to place a complaint regarding the enclosed letter.

I was married to Tom Snow Nov 25, 1979 and left him August 26 of 1986. During the last 2 years of the marriage he was asked repeatedly to treat me in a more humane and civil manner. He was told that I would have no other choice but to leave if we could not communicate and treat one another as best friends and as human beings. I asked him four times the summer of '85 to go with me to see a marriage counselor - He refused. In other words, the man had every chance possible to <u>help</u> save this marriage but refused to do so.

I am a professional person. I have worked for past nine years selling pharmaceuticals

Out of Control

to both medical doctors and veterinarians. Therefore, Mr. Snow knew that I could support myself.

In August of '86, I finally convinced Tom to see a marriage counselor. Tom was extremely threatened by seeing the counselor and a few days after seeing him started becoming very threatening towards me. I was awakened in the middle of the night with Tom pouring water over my head saying, "Get out of my bed!" He repeated the statement and proceeded to pour more water over my head. At this point, I came to the conclusion that I had done all I could do to help this man and that I was leaving at any cost - which I did a week later.

I don't mean to make a long story out of this but I wanted to give you a little background on the situation.

After I left, Tom became even more uncontrollable and threatened my life. I have been hit in the head, knocked over backward in chairs, dragged from my car into the house and thrown across the room. I have been choked, threatened

Get Out of My Bed

with a butcher knife and called every F"in nigger name in the book. I have very long hair which has been pulled until I was screaming. I have had my house broken into by this man after I left him. Needless to say, I had to make another decision which was extremely difficult but it came down to saving myself and my sanity - so I had to take an order of protection out on this person. And may God strike me dead I have never done anything to this man to deserve any of this treatment.

All I want is some peace and quiet in my life and to get on with some type of reasonably happy existence. I do not want any support. The legal matter only involves the disbursement of whatever debts and assets we have.

I filed for divorce Dec 9 of '86, we had a court date back in the summer and nothing could be agreed to, therefore it has to go before a judge. We had a court date Nov. 10 '89; the Judge was sick - therefore canceled. We had a court date of Dec 17, the enclosed letter was written. Now we have a court date of March 7.

Twice A Victim

Mr. Snow has been treated for hypertension and high blood high blood pressure most of his adult life. During our seven-year marriage, he has been treated by numerous doctors for this condition - three of which I will enclose the addresses and phone numbers for. He had been given numerous and different medications and has never stayed with one long enough for his body to adjust. We had a medicine cabinet full of different blood pressure and other medications, which he refused to take. During our marriage I asked him repeatedly to exercise with me, go for walks, anything to help him reduce his blood pressure. He always refused. I did all I could to persuade him to eat properly and take better care of himself. The man is his own worst enemy and always will be.

He has been hospitalized for his high blood pressure several times in the past 10 years. The latest of which was November 27 at St. Jude Hospital. Dr. Tomson has been the family doctor for many years. Tom was discharged from the hospital December 3. The letter was supposedly

Get Out of My Bed

written and dated Friday - Dec 4th, Tom was seen by individuals snowmobiling in the Cold Spring area that same weekend and he flew to Portugal on business that week. Not a man who is very ill I would say.

All I want is for someone to give me a break. I have suffered from the control of this man too long.

He will drag the affair out as long as he possibly can. Any last string, he can maintain to hold on to me in some insane way he will do and now the medical world has allowed him to do so for a few more months and maybe longer. Believe me - he is now laughing at both the medical and legal professions. He's an expert at passing the buck but I won't take this one sitting down. Our marital problems are no more a reason for his physical condition than Hitler's insanity and obsessions were due to hypertension. Is there anyone who can help me stop this man. All I want is a divorce and be rid of this person in my life. And I'll say it again - I know no one is perfect, but I don't deserve any of this.

Twice A Victim

The only thing accomplished by my letter was venting my own frustration. A new court date was set for March 7th.

Chapter 12
Twice a Victim

On Friday, March 4th I had an appointment to discuss the case with my attorney. During this short conference nothing was accomplished and he told me to come back the next day at 1:00 p.m. He informed me that Tom was going to be in his attorney's office and we were to call to determine if we could work something out before going to court on Monday. I said, "Great!" Who would ever think that your own attorney would flat out lie to you?

    I arrived at his office on Saturday, optimistic that some agreement might be made before going to court. When I arrived, he was flipping through some law books and stated that he was trying to find some information or a similar case that he could use especially concerning Tom's debts. We went over the debts and I mentioned to him that the dates on all the statements were May of 1987, when we had the deposition. I stated that these were invalid since the statements should be dated relevant to our separation date which was December 10, 1986. He agreed and said that Tom would have to come up with those statements and this would be discussed during court.

He made the phone call to Tom and his attorney, let it ring several times, and hung up. He said very nonchalantly, "Well, I guess they don't want to talk. They aren't there. We'll have to go to court." I was devastated. I just wanted to get it over with. I was both mentally and emotionally drained. Today I realize what easy prey I was for both the attorneys and my husband. I later learned that Tom and his attorney weren't in the office at all. My attorney, Jackson, had mentioned during our meeting on Saturday that his wife and children were out of town for the weekend. Could it be that he had nothing better to do than come into the office on a Saturday and make another $85.00 for a one-hour conference with me?

The next morning on Sunday, Jackson's assistant called me at home and stated that they had some new information and asked me to be at the courthouse at 10:00 a.m. the next day rather than 1:00 p.m.

When I arrived at the courthouse on Monday I was placed in a large room with Jackson's assistant. Tom

Get Out of My Bed

and his attorney were in another part of the building. I never saw either of them until we went before the judge to finalize the divorce. A dear friend was also there waiting to testify for me. Since no one had ever heard or seen Tom's abusive behavior, she would testify that I had spent a few nights at her home because I was afraid to be alone. But the two attorneys settled the case without going before the judge.

When Jackson arrived and we started discussing matters, he began to talk very negatively about the case. His attitude and tone were entirely different from what I had previously seen. He began throwing the copies of Tom's debts in front of me. One by one he asked, "Do you know anything about this?" I once again explained that I did not know where all this money was spent and I believed a great deal of it was borrowed during September, October, and November when we weren't living together before I filed. He stated, "Well, since the date on all these debts is before your separation date you are legally half responsible." We went round and round for two hours. I noticed that the date on these bills was December, which would be the appropriate legal date, not May of 1987. I asked if this was the new information that he had obtained over the weekend. He replied that it was, and that I was half responsible for all these debts in this state and that there was nothing he could do about it. Even his assistant asked, "What about all the money she had contributed to the marriage? Didn't that count for something?" He said that it didn't matter. The law was the law. I asked, "Well, why don't we let the judge make that decision?" Jackson replied, "If you go before a judge it will be worse." I asked him how it could be worse.

He kept saying that the only thing that mattered here is what the debts and assets were when I filed and that these debts far outweigh the assets. I have never felt more helpless than I did at that moment. If my own attorney was not going to help me, after all, I had already been through, then I had no hope at all. I was totally exhausted and after two hours of arguing, I gave in.

My own attorney literally handed me over on a silver platter. Tom took everything plus I owed him $7,000.00. He even talked me into half of the seven thousand going towards paying Tom's attorney. The only thing I got was my divorce and a few pieces of furniture.

From Thursday, March 3rd through Monday the 7th my attorney charged me a total of $1,035.50. On the one and only bill I received, this $1,035.50 was in

Get Out of My Bed

addition to the $1,000.00 that I had already given him up front for two days in court which I obviously didn't get. The billing from March 3rd through March 7th reads as follows:

3/04/88 – 1 hr. personal conf. w/Shirley $ 85.00

3/03/88 – Paralegal time, 2 hours 50.00

3/04/88 – Paralegal time, 1 hour 25.00

3/05/88 – Paralegal time, ½ hour 12.50

3/06/88 – Paralegal time, 1 hour 25.00

3/07/88 – Paralegal time, 6 hours 150.00

3/07/88 – Mileage Fee 8.00

3/05/88 – 1 hr. personal conf. w/Shirley 85.00

3/07/88 – 3 hrs. trial preparation 225.00

3/07/88 – 4 hours trial 340.00

When I was considering suing my attorney, I obtained a booklet entitled <u>The Lawyer's Code of Professional Responsibility</u> from the State Bar Association.

In the first chapter, entitled "A Lawyer Should Assist in Maintaining the Integrity and Competence of the Legal Profession" under DR 1-102 section, it reads that a lawyer "shall not engage in conduct involving dishonesty, fraud, deceit, or misrepresentation."

In the second chapter, entitled "A Lawyer Should Assist the Legal Profession in Fulfilling its Duty to Make Legal Counsel Available" under EC 2-19 it reads:

> EC 2-19 As soon as feasible after a lawyer has been employed, it is desirable that a clear agreement be reached with the client as to the basis of the fee charges to be made. Such a course will not only prevent later misunderstanding but will also work for good relations between the lawyer and the client. It is usually beneficial to reduce to writing the understanding of the parties regarding the fee, particularly when it is contingent. A lawyer should be mindful that many persons who desire to employ a lawyer may have had little or no experience with fee charges of lawyers, and for this reason, lawyers should explain fully to such persons the reasons for the particular fee arrangement proposed.

Get Out of My Bed

§

Chapter 6 is entitled "A Lawyer Should Represent a Client Competently." In this chapter under Disciplinary Rules it states that a lawyer shall not:

1. Handle a legal matter which he knows or should know that he is not competent to handle, without associating with him a lawyer who is competent to handle it.

2. Handle a legal matter without preparation adequate in the circumstances.

3. Neglect a legal matter entrusted to him.

§

A chapter entitled "A Lawyer Should Represent a Client Zealously Within the Bounds of the Law" contains the following paragraphs:

> EC 7-8 A lawyer should exert his best efforts to insure that decisions of his client are made only after the client has been informed of relevant considerations. A lawyer ought to initiate this decision-making process if the client does not do so. Advice of a lawyer to his client need not be confined to purely legal considerations. A lawyer

should advise his client of the possible effect of each legal alternative. A lawyer should bring to bear upon this decision-making process the fullness of his experience as well as his objective viewpoint. In assisting his client to reach a proper decision, it is often desirable for a lawyer to point out those factors which may lead to a decision that is morally just as well as legally permissible. He may emphasize the possibility of harsh consequences that might result from assertion of legally permissible positions. In the final analysis, however, the lawyer should always remember that the decision whether to forego legally available objectives or methods because of non-legal factors is ultimately for the client and not for himself. In the event that the client in a non-adjudicatory matter insists upon a course of conduct that is contrary to the judgment and advice of the lawyer but not prohibited by Disciplinary Rules, the lawyer may withdraw from the employment.

EC 7-9 In the exercise of his professional judgment on those decisions which are for his determination in the handling of a legal matter, a lawyer should always act in a manner consistent with the best interests of his client. However, when an action in the best interest of his client seems to him to be unjust, he may ask his client for permission to forego such action.

§

In my search for help, I came upon a group known as HALT, which is the nation's oldest and largest legal reform organization. I acquired a booklet entitled <u>Directory of Lawyers Who Sue Lawyers</u> through this agency. This booklet lists four types of discipline that agencies who police lawyer conduct can mete out. They are:

#1 Private Reprimand. A written or oral chastising of the lawyer. It is not made public.

#2 Public Reprimand. A public notice listing the lawyer's misconduct, usually published in a bar association journal.

#3 Suspension. Suspending a lawyer's license to practice law in a given state for a specified time, ranging from a few days to several years.

Twice A Victim

#4 Disbarment. Removing a lawyer from practicing law in a specified state for at least five years, usually with a hearing required for re-admission.

§

In 1989, when this booklet was published, it stated that more than 70,000 complaints are filed each year, but only about two percent are ever publicly disciplined.

Each state has a lawyer-run agency to which these complaints are sent and processed. In 1989 in seventeen states these agencies were run directly by the state bar association Their only function is to police violations of the state's "Code of Professional Responsibility" based on a model written by the American Bar Association. This is the same booklet that I previously referred to.

As I personally found out, it is extremely difficult to find an attorney who will sue another. The time, effort, and money it takes even to search for one is big enough aggravation.

My advice to you is that if you need to hire an attorney you first obtain a copy of The Lawyer's Code of Professional Responsibility.

Get Out of My Bed

After the legal case is over and done, you might as well use the pages of the <u>Lawyer's Code of Professional Responsibility</u> for tissue paper. At least if you don't put all your trust in this person and you half-way know the type of system you're dealing with, your chances of getting an honest attorney will increase. I would make sure that my attorney knew that I was familiar with the lawyer code and that he/she knew exactly what you expected of him. That's only being fair and that's the way it should be. If he/she doesn't want to take your case, then that's fine. You are probably much better off. Your odds should increase greatly in finding an attorney who is capable and willing to work for your better interest. That's his job.

I was already an emotional disaster from my relationship with Tom.

But now I had to deal with the reality that my own attorney had been nothing more than a detriment to me. I would have been better off to represent myself.

I called my counselor from the spouse abuse clinic and told her the outcome of the divorce. She had recommended Jackson to me. Her parting words to me were that I was now twice a victim.

I had to keep myself busy and preoccupied in order to avoid breaking down. But I found myself crying

Twice a Victim

many times while driving between sales calls. My emotions could also be rather embarrassing.

I had a dental appointment in June and I cried the entire time the technician was cleaning my teeth. She became upset because she thought she was hurting me. I kept reassuring her that she wasn't hurting me at all and that I was simply emotional because of personal problems.

One morning towards the end of July, I was standing in front of the mirror putting my make-up on for work. A half-moon prism of light began to blur my vision over one eye. I was petrified. I called an eye doctor and was able to see him that morning.

Once again, I couldn't stop crying. The technician made a notation on the medical file to treat with tender loving care. The diagnosis was that I had a type of migraine headache which could have been caused by eye strain and stress. I was given something for pain and told to get some rest.

Chapter 13
Tom's List of Debts

When I left Tom at the end of August, he had just given his notice to his employer that he was quitting because he had a job offer from a company located an hour from Cold Springs. I have no idea as to what happened between Tom and his new employer, but they reneged on their offer. Tom tried to sue the company, but the case was thrown out of court on the first hearing.

He begged his former employer to take him back, but they refused. Needless to say, this put an even greater strain on an already volatile situation. Not only had he lost his wife, he now had no job. I knew there was no way I could file for divorce until he found a job and became more emotionally stable. I was terrified of him and the only way I knew to keep safe was to patronize him until things became more sane.

Tom's List of Debts

I did everything possible to be his friend and keep the relationship civil. I insisted on his seeing the marriage counselor with me, which he did on two occasions. After that, he refused to see him again. He kept saying we didn't need anyone else to solve our problems. I knew our personal relationship was over, but I wanted Tom to see a counselor for his own peace of mind. I begged him to go for counseling, but he would not hear of it.

He began to threaten my life and his own, which I became very concerned about. I did whatever possible to keep him calm, but most of the time I just tried to avoid him as much as possible.

He found another job in a few weeks and started spending time on the road. I had overnights in my own job, so this helped to keep some distance between us.

He complained about money constantly and began threatening me with bankruptcy. But although he said he couldn't make ends meet his actions were sometimes very contradictory to what he said. He had a later model company car to drive, which was supplied by his new employer, but he purchased a new 1987 Dodge pick-up. I never dared say a word to him about anything because, first of all, I knew that I wouldn't get anywhere, and secondly I avoided an argument under all circumstances. Any conflicting conversations usually led to one of Tom's outbursts and I tried to avoid those totally. This was when I felt my safety was in jeopardy.

As the weeks passed and I felt that financially he was doing better, I started thinking more about filing for divorce. I had done everything I could to keep the peace, but his outbursts continued and I decided that there was no reason to postpone the inevitable. On December 10th I filed for legal separation. I had no intentions of hurting this man financially or otherwise. I simply knew that if I didn't get away from him he would totally destroy me emotionally. My self-esteem at this moment was close to zero. But to this day I know his story is that I almost destroyed him.

I had hoped that we could do this amicably, but no such luck. I'm not a greedy person, I just wanted something to show for seven years of marriage and hard work. But the attorneys and Tom had something much different in mind.

When I left Tom in August I was aware that he had some pretty high balances on charge cards. If I had to guess I would have said that it was around $10,000.00, which to me is a lot of money. But when I

Tom's List of Debts

filed for divorce Tom presented a list of personal debts totaling $52,439.58 and as we arrived at the courthouse he presented another $17,000.00 which he had taken from an insurance policy which brought the total to $69,439.58.

I created a list of Tom's debt totaling $52,439.58. I took the dollar amounts from the monthly billing copies Tom presented for proof of our debts. From this information, I was able to determine how much money Tom had taken in cash advances versus purchases on his charge cards.

The following is as close to an explanation for the debts that I can get from anyone, including the banks he borrowed the money from.

#1. This is a loan taken out for a pick-up truck purchased by Tom a couple of years before I left. We used the truck quite often but Tom had turned the truck over to his two sons and it was my understanding before I left that they were making the payments although the loan was still in Tom's name. Tom listed this debt as $5,242.05.

#2. This money was used to purchase furniture for our home. The balance was $596.56.

Get Out of My Bed

#3. This was a bank loan originally for $3,500.00 which was used to pay for the six acres we built our cabin on in Cold Springs. The collateral used for this loan was stock which I had earned through my employment. In the fall of 1986 when we were not living together but not yet legally separated, I gave Tom permission to cash in the stock and pay off the loan which was then $1,964.32. The stock was valued at $3,200.00 and I told him to keep the remaining $1,200.00 and use it wherever he saw fit.

#4. This was a Visa Charge Card on which Tom had $2,014.55 in cash advances and $353.05 in purchases.

#5. A Master Charge on which Tom had taken $4,835.57 in cash advances. There were no purchases.

#6. This was a Visa Card with $1,921.29 in cash advances.

#7. A Master Charge account with $1,184.16 in cash advances and $1,108.33 in purchases.

Tom's List of Debts

#8. A Master Charge with $2,865.51 in cash advances and no purchases.

#9. A Master Charge account with $112.79 in cash advances and $1,550.15 in purchases.

#10. This is a Visa Card with $1,836.21 in cash advances and no purchases.

#11. A charge account with $1,100.05 in advances.

#12. A charge card with $355.15 in cash advances and $1,234.55 in purchases.

#13. Credit card with $4,603.99 in cash advances.

#14. A financial service company with $750.33 in cash borrowed at the time we legally separated. Tom listed $1,019.28.

#15. Debt of $384.48. I was unable to determine the source of this debt.

#16. Credit card with $1,787.46 in cash advances and $19.51 in purchases.

#17. A Visa Card with no purchases and $4,751.90 in cash advances.

Get Out of My Bed

#18. A Master Charge with $5,848.79 in cash advances and no purchases.

#19. A debt for $112.00. I was unable to determine the source for this debt.

#20. A Master Card with no purchases and $4,649.88 in cash advances.

#21. Attorney fee for $288.00 incurred before we separated. This was a legal cost for putting our Creek Road property in my name in case anything happened to Tom. Obviously, since we acquired the property while married, this had no bearing on the outcome of our divorce case. It appears that nothing else did either. At least not in my favor.

At the time I filed for divorce, Tom had a total of $43,579.78 on charge accounts with $38,717.63 in cash and $4,862.15 in purchases.

The only charge card my name was on was item #7 for $2,292.49. I did not use any of these cards because I had a Master Charge and Visa card of my own.

Tom and I had a signed and notarized agreement stating that he would pay the Society card when he sold the Harrisville property. I knew the house was

Tom's List of Debts

on the market and called the real estate company, periodically. It was sold in October 1989. I waited two months for the card balance to be paid.

Once again, Tom was going to show me he was still in control.

The payoff for the house was $74,333.00, and he sold it for $110,000. I eventually had to take him to small claims court. Obviously, the judge ruled in my favor. Tom still did not pay the balance and I had to file an income execution at the county courthouse. It stated, "pay in 20 days or your wages will be garnished."

That got his attention. He called and asked me to give him 90 days. I'm surprised the phone line did not melt from my screams. I received a check the following week.

I filed December 10, 1985. It took me until January 1991 to separate myself from him financially.

If your husband or wife owns a charge card in his/her name only and you try to obtain information on where or when the money is being spent, I hope you have better luck than I did. I could get no cooperation from the banks or lenders since my name was not on the account. I was told that I was not responsible for this debt, but my "own" attorney held me responsible-

Get Out of My Bed

-obviously because that was the easiest and quickest way out. He told me that the state in which I lived held that everything was 50/50, whether it be a debt or an asset. Even before the court date, my attorney never asked me to try to obtain information on any of these debts, nor did he pursue it himself.

On the court date, the two attorneys took all the debts minus the assets and informed me that I owed Tom $7,000.00. Our assets consisted of the equity we had accumulated in our home in Harrisville and the value of our Creek Road property which was paid for. Between the two of them, I would estimate the equity to be about $65,000.00. I realize now how emotionally unstable I was at that time. I could not have fought my way out of a paper bag. Plus, I never dreamed my own attorney would allow this to happen. When I look back, it was the most insane situation one could ever imagine. I'm the one who was forced to leave my home and yet I still tried to get help for Tom. I was the perfect puppet-on-a-string for both attorneys and Tom. I was nothing more than a scapegoat.

I never tried to hurt Tom in any way, but I knew if I didn't get out of that situation all I had to look forward to was a very miserable life.

Tom's List of Debts

Unfortunately, when Tom also found himself without a job, that compounded the already volatile situation. My question is this: How much of this money was deliberately borrowed between August 26th and December 10th when we were not living as husband and wife but had not yet filed for legal separation? Could it be that while I was trying to reason with him and keep the peace, he was borrowing every penny he could, so that he and his attorney could hopefully present a very one-sided case against me?

Chapter 14
My Monetary Contributions

I feel that my financial contributions to our marriage were considerable over the seven years we were together. When we were first married my salary was $14,700.00 with a possible $1,000.00 to $1,500.00 in commission. From the beginning of the marriage, I deposited $400.00 per month or $200.00 per pay period to Tom's checking account. This $400.00 was intended to help with household expenses. I gave each deposit slip to Tom, and I did not keep a copy. Therefore, there was no way to prove that I actually did contribute this $400.00 each month. Always keep a copy of any deposits you make towards the household or marriage. You just may need them some time to prove what you contributed. And believe me that's all the attorneys in my case were interested in, and I'm sure that is the case in most divorce courts. My attorney could not have cared less as to why I was leaving. Over a six-year

My Monetary Contributions

period that I contributed the $400.00/month to Tom's checking account, that comes to $28,000.00.

I also purchased 90% of our groceries and other household items. If you estimate $70.00 per week for these expenses that would be another $22,400.00. If you feel you may be seeking legal advice for a divorce ever, then start saving all grocery receipts and all others that show you are contributing to the marriage and household. I also provided for the personal needs of my two daughters, which I have no estimate for.

When we purchased the first six acres in Cold Springs we borrowed the $3,600.00 and I put up stock I had acquired through my work for collateral.

When we began building our weekend home, I borrowed $3,000.00 from my credit union. We used this money for building materials and the payment was taken out directly from my paychecks. It took me over three years to pay it back.

About a year and a half after we were married we decided to purchase a home because we needed the benefit of taking the interest on our income taxes. We purchased a home which was priced at $110,000.00 and our payments were approximately $800.00 per month. We had been paying $600.00 per month rent. At the time it seemed like a good choice. But later when

Get Out of My Bed

we began to have serious problems and I moved to our cabin, our other home became more of a burden. Fortunately, Tom was able to lease it with an option to purchase which worked fairly well.

In June of 1984, almost two years before I would leave, Tom and I won a Caribbean cruise for two through my work. I had hoped Tom would go with me and felt this might help save our relationship, but he flatly refused. The company was generous enough to give me a check for $2,000.00 instead of the trip. The money was used to purchase more building materials for our Cold Springs home. When I was searching through my canceled checks I found another $1,450.00 that I wrote for building materials.

In January of 1986, I walked out our driveway in Cold Springs and saw a for sale sign on the undeveloped property across the road. Tom did not seem to be at all concerned about the situation, but I felt we had no choice but to purchase the six acres. We were located on a dirt road in a rural area and I valued our privacy highly. After a lengthy discussion with Tom, he still had no interest and I was amazed at his attitude. I contacted the owner, myself, and made the $850.00 down payment and paid $60.00 per month on

My Monetary Contributions

the property. I made the last payment in the spring of 1992. I also paid the $270.00 attorney fee for the transfer of title.

During November of 1986 when Tom and I were separated but not legally, he constantly complained about money. He had found another job but was always threatening me with bankruptcy. As I previously stated, I had put up stock as collateral when we purchased the first six acres in Cold Springs. There was still $2,000.00 owed on this loan, which Tom was making the monthly payments. I told him to call the bank and cash in the stock. Therefore we could pay off the loan and he could keep the remaining $1,200.00, which he did.

We were legally separated on the 10th of December, 1986. Our home in Harrisville was being leased, but Tom was still contributing $300.00 per month to the payment on this property, which he constantly complained about. We also had a second mortgage, which was due in September of 1987, when I was trying unsuccessfully to get a divorce. My attorney advised me to pay half this second mortgage in order to, in his words, "show good faith." Therefore, I paid out another $2,500.00.

Get Out of My Bed

I also paid the property taxes for Cold Springs in February of 1986, November 1986, and January 1987, which came to a total of $635.00.

So, what I'm saying here is that I contributed substantially to our finances, not to mention the fact that I worked like a man besides my husband, whether it was building our weekend home, splitting wood, or some other chore. The estimate of my monetary contributions came to $65,705.00. I might add that I also put my daughter through college from September of 1985 through August of 1989.

I'm not blowing my own horn at all. Many wives and girlfriends contribute to their mates greatly. But I am saying that if you even suspect a divorce some time down the road, please be able to document and prove your contributions because that's what it all comes down to--dollars and cents.

Chapter 15
The Fee Dispute

When I first approached my attorney, Dick Jackson, regarding the handling of my divorce case, he quoted me a flat $650.00 fee for a relatively simple settlement. I tried to be optimistic about the cost and time it would take for a divorce, but I had both attorneys and my husband working against the possibility of anything being sensible or fair.

Now that it's all over and done, it's quite apparent that my own attorney lied to me on numerous occasions and could not have cared less about my financial welfare or psychological well-being. I was nothing more than a means to an end and that end was only to make more money. It's extremely depressing to think that there are many of these people out there and that they can have your life in their hands and you have very little control, if any, on the outcome.

Get Out of My Bed

In December of 1987, a year after I filed, I became very concerned about how my attorney was handling the case and I made an appointment to see him. I asked several questions about the case, one of which was, "What is the worst outcome?" And the other, "What is the best?" His answer was that the worst was that everything would be sold and we would divide anything that was left over after paying any debts. The best outcome would be if we bought out my husband's half of the Creek Road property and he could have the home which had been our permanent residence. Obviously, neither of these scenarios came to pass.

During this meeting, I also asked if I owed him any more money since I had already given him $1,650.00. The $650.00 was his initial fee for a simple case and the $1,000.00 he had requested to cover two days in court since it appeared we could not settle otherwise. He told me no, I did not owe any more money, and that, if anything, I was ahead of the $1,000.00 because that would cover the court cost. I never got my two days in court because the day I arrived at the courthouse I was put into a large room with my attorney's female assistant and my attorney. For the next two hours, Jackson threw copies of Tom's debts in front of me and said that I was 50% responsible for all of these bills. I kept telling him that I didn't borrow it and neither

The Fee Dispute

did I spend it. He said that it didn't matter because it was borrowed before December 10th, 1986 when I filed for divorce. No one but Tom will ever know how much of that $69,000.00 was borrowed between August 26th and December 10th, the period of time Tom was threatening me with anything he could dream up if I went through with the divorce. The bottom line is that Tom and his attorney used the law to get me. If I had filed immediately after leaving he wouldn't have had the opportunity to get as far in debt as he did.

I received a bill for an additional $1,000 from Jackson, which I refused to pay.

I filed a formal complaint with the Knoxville Judiciary Board regarding this extra charge. A date was set for Jackson and me to testify before the Fee Dispute Committee.

Jackson was trying to sue me through Small Claims court for this additional $1,000 but after we met with the committee he withdrew the case. In addition to not having to pay him more money, I certainly embarrassed him in front of his peers. I informed them how he had lied to me and how he had done little to nothing to help me in my divorce case.

Chapter 16
Happy Trails

After my divorce, I continued to live in the Cold Springs area. I loved the little house I was renting and I continued my pharmaceutical sales position. I don't think I have to tell you how much I enjoyed having Tom out of my life. He had taken an engineering position out of the area, so I did not have to worry about our paths crossing.

But, on one occasion, our paths did cross. I was picking up a few groceries in a small store in a neighboring town. I came around the end of an aisle and there he was. And, he had not seen me. I immediately checked out my few items and the young man bagging groceries asked me "Paper or plastic?" I barely whispered, "paper." He must have thought something was wrong with me because he carried my purchase to my car. I got out of there as quickly as possible. That feeling of

Happy Trails

anxiety and fear was overwhelming just from seeing him. I always considered myself as an emotionally strong person, but Tom had literally programmed me to be terrified of him.

Today, I am in a very positive relationship. I feel loved, respected and appreciated. We live on a small farm and enjoy our animals. Life is relatively calm and peaceful.

It has been 30 years since I wrote: "Get Out of My Bed". It took me a long time to complete the manuscript. I, then, packed it away in a box and went on with my life. I had always entertained the thought of finding a publisher but never pursued it. They say "Timing is everything". That is certainly the case here. I accidentally made contact with my publisher through an internet marketing course.

Unfortunately, Domestic Abuse has been a social issue since human existence and this book is still relevant.

I want this memoir to be a wake-up call to both men and women. Please be very cautious regarding your intimate relationships. It could become your worst nightmare. God Bless and Happy Trails.

Get Out of My Bed

BJ and Shirley on their snow mobile.

Happy Trails...

Message From Shirley Rose

"You have to protect yourself and your children from an abusive relationship.

As women, we nurture and try to make things right. We think we can make someone happy and make their lives better. But, sometimes, you cannot help them and you become trapped. In my memoir, you will see how Tom gradually manipulated me with his mental abuse. My life became a series of explanations and responses to the man in control. Please learn from my experience, do not become the abused."

Shirley Rose graduated from Appalachian State in 1972 with a BA degree in Sociology/Criminal Justice. She has spent her life building a career in sales, becoming an entrepreneur, raising two daughters and enjoying her passion for horses and snowmobiling. Shirley currently resides on a farm in the foothills of North Carolina.

You can follow and get in touch with Shirley Rose by visiting her website: http://www.shirleywrose.com.

Get Out of My Bed